always alex

my story

always alex
my story

alex best

JOHN BLAKE

Published byJohn Blake Publishing Ltd,
3, Bramber Court, 2 Bramber Road,
London W14 9PB, England

www.blake.co.uk

First published in hardback in 2005

ISBN 1 84454 099 5

British Library Cataloguing-in-Publication Data:

A catalogue record for this book is available from the British Library.

Design by www.envydesign.co.uk

Printed in Great Britain by William Clowes

1 3 5 7 9 10 8 6 4 2

Papers used by John Blake Publishing are natural, recyclable
products made from wood grown in sustainable forests.
The manufacturing processes conform to the environmental
regulations of the country of origin.

Every attempt has been made to contact the relevant copyright-holders,
but some were unobtainable. We would be grateful if the appropriate
people could contact us.

Some names have been changed for legal reasons.

To Mum, Dad and Jo, for their
continuing love and support.

CONTENTS

Acknowledgements

Thanks to H, Ian Monk and
Julie-Lynn Savage. Also to all my family and
everyone and Blake Publishing.

CHAPTER ONE

SURREY SWEETHEART

I'm a romantic at heart, and because of this I love the story of how my parents first met. One night they were both in the same pub in a little Derbyshire village – my mum a pretty blonde local girl, my dad a dark-haired stranger. Suddenly across the crowded room their eyes locked and, cliché of clichés, it was love at first sight – a real Romeo and Juliet moment.

Ironically, my mum had heard all about my dad because her best friend was totally in love with him. In fact, Mum was so fed up of listening to her friend go on and on about this 'wonderful Adrian' that she declared, 'Oh my God! I've had enough of hearing his name, I never want to set eyes on the man!' When she did, and found out who he was, she was stunned. Fortunately, her best friend got over her infatuation pretty quickly, leaving the way free for my mum.

But Mum didn't have it all her own way. I think she

imagined that because she and Dad were so in love a proposal of marriage would quickly follow. But my dad found it quite hard to express his feelings and three years on from their first meeting he still hadn't popped the question. Mum was fed up of waiting. At the grand old age of 25 she already felt that time was running out for her, so one day she said, 'That's it! I'm going to go off and become an air hostess and travel the world if he won't marry me.' It's ironic that I had exactly the same desire when one of my relationships wasn't going well. I suppose it is the ultimate way of flouncing away, though boarding a plane is a little more dramatic than simply slamming the door or stamping your foot. It didn't really work for me, but it definitely did for my mum.

My grandmother took my dad to one side and had a quiet word with him. 'She is serious, you know,' she said. 'She's going to do it and she'll meet some gorgeous pilot and you will have missed your chance.' Finally my dad was galvanised into action and he proposed to my mother. She never did become an air hostess, but I don't think she regrets it for a second.

Thirty-five years on, my parents have the happiest, most rock-solid marriage I have ever known. In all those years I have never once heard them argue. My mum accepts that my dad isn't at all romantic – he never buys her flowers or Valentine's cards. If she's ever received a card with a heart on it, it's only because my sister or I have brought it for him to give to her, saying, 'For goodness sake, Dad, show some emotion!' Of course, he does show emotion – but in his own way. Recently, my mum said to me, 'Your dad has never brought me flowers, but that's not what matters – he's a true and wonderful husband and who needs the presents if you've got that?' Who indeed!

I couldn't be happier that my parents' marriage is so strong, but it's been a hard thing to measure up to sometimes. I always imagined that my marriage would be the same – that we would stay together forever, have children, have a love that was unbreakable. When things went wrong for me – and they did so in a big way – it was hard not to feel that I had failed somehow. I had the perfect example of what marriage could be, so why was mine falling apart? I can't exactly blame my parents for being happy, though, can I?

A year after my parents married, I – Alexandra Macadam Pursey – arrived. I get my unusual middle name from my great-grandfather, who invented Tarmac. Construction and business is in our genes and today my dad is a company director for an industrial belting manufacturer. I didn't exactly follow in his footsteps!

My parents came from very different backgrounds – Dad from an upper-class family and Mum from a working-class family (her father was the local village postmaster). At one time my father's family had been very wealthy, and they had even owned an enormous family estate in Bristol, one of the biggest in Europe – Madonna eat your heart out! But unfortunately I didn't get to live out my fantasy of being the lady of the manor. When my grandfather died, the estate had to be sold off to pay death duties. One time I went down there to have a peek. Rather unnervingly, the local pub was stuffed with pictures of my grandfather and great-grandfather and as I pulled in to look at the house, now a posh hotel, my friend pointed out that we were on Pursey Drive! So something of my family lingered on.

But, despite the family wealth, Dad didn't have a very happy childhood. His mother was quite a cold, emotionally detached woman, his father was weak and in her shadow and if they loved their children they didn't know how to show it. Dad was mainly brought up by a succession of nannies and then dispatched to boarding school as soon as he was old enough to go, leaving my beautiful and glamorous grandmother free to lunch at the Ritz and shop for designer clothes. There was no solace to be found at school either, as it was one of those grim, forbidding institutions, which still had fagging and where bullying was rife. It was the kind of place where it was considered character-building to make children suffer, so every day the boys would have to swim in the outside swimming pool, which was filled with icy seawater. Dad would frequently have to stay there during the holidays as well, because my grandmother didn't want him around – she probably didn't want her social diary interrupted.

Fortunately for my sister and me, Dad wasn't turned into a dysfunctional emotional wreck by his upbringing. If anything, it had the opposite effect, and he devoted himself to making our childhood as happy as possible. My mum came from a very warm, loving family, so she knew all about showing emotion and making people feel loved. It might not be fashionable to say it, but I had an idyllic childhood; I have no skeletons hidden away and I can honestly say that I knew total, unconditional love. We're a very close family – I've always been able to tell my parents and sister Jo everything, and they have always been there for me. Over the years I have been able to depend on them and they have been my salvation through some very difficult times.

As soon as she had me, Mum gave up work and devoted herself to being a full-time mother. I see her as such a positive role model, because she loved being a mum and was so good at it. She never had any doubt that she wanted to have a career as well, as being a mother completely fulfilled her. It is exactly how I want to be when I have children.

I was brought up in Cheam, a pretty little village in Surrey. Looking back, it was an ideal place to live, as it was surrounded by beautiful countryside but was also within half an hour of London. Mum always said that she wanted us to experience every aspect of life and to try as many different things as possible. So, from a very young age she got us playing sports – tennis, swimming and riding – and was forever taking us off on trips to London, to places such as the Natural History Museum or the Tower of London.

My home life was blissfully happy, but primary school wasn't such a great experience for me – particularly the later years, when the pressure was on to pass the Eleven

Plus. I was in a large class and I often felt that only the really bright children got the teacher's attention. The rest of us were left to get on with it – sink or swim, and I was starting to sink. Maths was my biggest problem; I had never been very good at it, even with the extra coaching paid for by my parents. Because I was starting to struggle, the school kept me back a year, which was a disaster for me. I started tuning out of lessons and falling behind. Worse still, I stopped eating. I had never had a huge appetite but, now that I felt so unhappy at school, I had even less of one. I quickly became quite dramatically thin – not that I'd had much weight to lose in the first place. At the age of eleven I was wearing clothes that would have fitted an eight-year-old. Finally my mum sat me down and said, 'If you don't eat this bowl of porridge, you're going to die.' It might not have worked with a lot of other little girls in the same situation, but it worked for me.

I took my Eleven Plus… and failed. So, instead of getting into the girls' grammar school, I got a place at one of the worst comprehensives in the area. I don't think I minded too much – anything would have been better than my grim Victorian primary school. But that was definitely not how my parents felt. They decided they would send me to a private school, thinking that the smaller classes and greater attention would build up my confidence again. This was not a decision to be taken lightly, and they would have to find a way of making sacrifices to pay. Although my dad's family had once been wealthy, the family money was long gone; we were by no means badly off, but we certainly weren't rolling in it.

So I got a place at Greenacre School for Girls. Right from the start, I adored it. The only downside was the horrendous uniform! Green featured heavily. We had to wear a Kermit the Frog green jumper, a pale-green shirt with a Peter Pan collar and a green A-line skirt that had to hang below the knee. Socks had to be beige and up to the knee, to ensure that absolutely no flesh was on show. We even had 'regulation' shoes in brown or black from Clarks. No wonder our nickname was 'kermits' or 'boogies'. Confronted with such an outfit, Carrie Bradshaw would have fainted. I chose to bend the rules: my skirt mysteriously became shorter than everyone else's; my socks came over my knee so they resembled stockings and I ditched the Clarks shoes for Doc Martens. Make-up was strictly forbidden, but I wore bright green mascara and lip-gloss – well, I thought to myself, at least it matched my jumper.

It was quite a strict school and I often found myself in trouble, though never for anything really serious – mainly for giggling and being silly in class. And the rules weren't just for inside the school building – one night I was perched on a bin outside McDonald's in Sutton High Street, eating a burger – as you do when you are fifteen and haven't got anywhere else to go – and one of my teachers caught me. I wasn't even in school uniform, but she was still appalled. 'Girls from Greenacre School do not sit on bins outside McDonald's on Sutton High Street eating burgers!' Oh crikey, I thought, I hope this doesn't mean she's going to send me to the headmistress. Miss Haggerty was a formidable woman. She had iron-grey hair, cut short like a man's, and her face was a stranger to make-up. She really ought to have invested in some electrolysis for her whiskers. But you never felt like laughing when you were summoned before her. Quite early on in my school career I developed a cunning plan for avoiding a telling-off from Miss Haggerty. There were two areas outside her office: the naughty zone – where you waited for the reprimand in fear and trepidation – and the sick zone – where you would wait for your parents to pick you up if you were unwell. More often than not after I'd been sent to Miss Haggerty I would sit instead in the sick zone and when she marched past I would do a great imitation of being at death's door. She would pause and say, 'I do hope you feel better soon.' I'd manage a feeble 'Thank you', wait till she was safely out of sight and race back gleefully to my classmates. I must have gained a bit of a reputation as a naughty girl, though, because on one occasion there was a rumour going round the school that certain pupils were sniffing Tippex, and I was summoned to see Miss Haggerty. I was outraged and for once my protestations of innocence were true. I assured Miss Haggerty that I had never succumbed to the temptation of the correcting fluid and she believed me.

I would say I was probably an average student; I left school with eight GCSEs, which I think is pretty respectable. I probably could have done better, but I wasn't the most studious girl in the school, even though I wanted to do well because I knew my mum and dad were making sacrifices to send me there. I started out working hard, but by the time I came to take my GCSEs my work ethic had taken a bit of a knock – I was becoming more preoccupied with my social life and with boys. Art was my all-time favourite subject. In fact, one of my ambitions back then was to be a fashion designer. I was also keen on English and History, as I love finding out about people. But I had let everything slip except my Art. I was faced with a stark choice of either putting everything into my Art coursework and hoping to get a place at art school or dropping Art and doing some serious catching up with my other subjects. I dropped Art, reluctantly, and frantically tried to get up to speed with English. Shamefully, I didn't have time to read my set texts for my coursework, so I had to watch *To Kill A Mockingbird* and *Romeo And Juliet* on video! I managed to get a grade 'A' though – maybe one day I'll read them...

Sport was a big thing at our school and luckily for me I was very sporty. We gels played lacrosse, which is a much more violent version of hockey – a kind of hockey in the air. Instead of hitting a ball on the ground you have to hurl it from your lacrosse stick, which has a net at the top. It was ferocious; tackling would take place mid-air as you whacked your opponent's net trying to get possession of the ball; frequently, dirty tactics were involved, and ankles and heads would get a good whack too. Our goalie would have to be got up like Darth

Vader, complete with helmet, visor and pads covering every inch of her body, making it practically impossible for her to move. Having played the game, I definitely believe women are the stronger sex – the viciousness of lacrosse would have grown men weeping.

I was also a very strong swimmer, and by the age of eleven was swimming for Surrey. Mum and Dad were always keen for my sister and me to do as many activities as possible, though I'm sure one of the reasons they got us swimming was to keep us out of trouble – i.e. away from boys! From about the age of nine to thirteen the weeks went by in a haze of chlorine and endless lengths while I swam for Wandsworth Dolphins. We would train three nights a week, leaving my parents free to meet up with their friends and have dinner, while we ploughed up and down the pool. Saturdays were gala days, and we even had training on Sunday. In between I had to fit in my schoolwork and looking after my pony, Bamber. And, of course, there was my growing interest in boys.

By the time I was thirteen, swimming had fallen by the wayside after I broke my arm really badly while on holiday in Corfu. I had even waved goodbye to the pony. At the weekends I wanted to go out and see my friends. I had important places to go, like the youth club or hanging around outside McDonald's or discos, and couldn't devote myself to mucking out with quite the same enthusiasm. (It's OK – Bamber went to a good home!)

I might have been at an all-girls school, but that in no

way curtailed my social life. I was popular at school and had a group of eight friends, with four of us being particularly close. Every weekend there would be parties or sleep-overs at friends' houses or discos to go to. And my friends' houses were big, expensive pads. I was by no means a pauper, but I did long to have a mansion with an impressive drive, as many of them did, rather than a pleasant semi-detached house with a nice garden. That said, the loss hardly scarred me for life!

I was still friendly with the group of boys I knew from primary school. They ended up going to the local private boys' school, and it was with them that my friends would socialise, holding joint discos and parties. It was with one of them, too, that I had my first proper kiss – Matthew Robinson, in the kitchen, on my thirteenth birthday. I thought it was a disgusting experience, made worse by my dad walking in halfway through. It wasn't a good omen for the relationship, and within a week Matthew had chucked me – only to go out with my best friend! Then he chucked her and asked me out again! The cheek! (But I said yes.) He carried on toying with our affections for several months, seeing one of us then the other, until finally we got a bit of girl power. 'Next time he chucks you and asks me out,' I said to my friend, 'I'll say no, and you must do the same.' We made a solemn pact and stood firm when he tried to wheedle his way back into our hearts. He moved on to someone else and so did we. I'd have a slow dance to 'Careless Whisper' with one of the other boys from the group, go out on a date with him

– we'd have coffee or if we were really daring go to Spudulike – and that would be it. I didn't meet anyone I felt anything particularly strongly for until, at the age of fifteen, I fell for Daniel, my bit of rough.

We met at the local youth club. Daniel didn't go to the posh private school like the other boys I knew; he went to the sink comprehensive I nearly ended up at. He was very good looking, with dark-blond hair and brown eyes, but best of all in my book he looked a little bit dangerous. Daniel wasn't like the clean-cut boys I knew. He smoked pot, was as common as anything, came from a family of hard nuts and I just knew my parents would hate him.

For a brief time he became my boyfriend. We snogged passionately outside the youth club, and stared dreamily into each other's eyes over our French fries. Mind you, he might not have intended to look dreamy as he did have a bit of a lazy eye, which only added to his charm as far as I was concerned.

One Saturday night I arranged to meet him for a date. I told my parents that I was at my friend's house but instead Daniel picked a few of us up at the end of my road, driving a bright-yellow Ford Fiesta. I do remember thinking as I got in that it was a little strange that he was driving because he was only 15, but didn't think to say anything. We stopped to fill up with petrol and all of a sudden a police car pulled up behind us, blue lights flashing. Daniel's criminal instinct must have kicked in, because he jumped back into the car and drove off at high speed, with the boys in blue in hot pursuit. The chase didn't last long; within a few miles he had admitted defeat and we were all being loaded into the meat wagon. Daniel had stolen the car.

'Please can I go home?' I asked the officer as soon as we got to the station and Daniel had been marched away.

'Not yet, young lady, you're an accessory to the crime – TDA: "taking and driving away"!' Oh lordy! It was time to play the posh card. When it was my turn to be interviewed by the Chief Constable I was as polite and charming as possible. No, sir, I really didn't realise the car was stolen. I'm so sorry that I got into it. I will never let anything like this happen again...

By now my dad had been notified and had turned up. He was completely mortified, never having set foot in a police station before. The combined force of my very respectable dad, my impeccable manners and the fact that I went to such a 'nice' school prompted the police to let me off with a caution. I was obviously a 'decent' girl. What on earth had I been doing with his sort? I shrugged meekly and was sent home – to have the riot act read to me by my parents.

My passion for my bit of rough died that night and I chucked Daniel on the phone the next time we spoke. For good measure my parents banned me from ever seeing him again and I was grounded for a month. I accepted my punishment; I knew I had been in the wrong and within a few weeks the whole incident had been forgotten, though I have to admit whenever I see a bright-yellow car now it does make me a bit queasy.

I really didn't have many battles with my parents

when I was growing up – the biggest bone of contention between us was that my dad always wanted me back home earlier than any of my friends. I was expected to be home at ten o'clock on the dot at the weekends when I was fifteen and woe betide me if I wasn't. Dad would be waiting at the end of the drive tapping his watch, which did nothing for my street cred. Other than that, my parents were pretty laid-back. They let me get on with being a teenager, experimenting with my appearance and inflicting my taste in music on them. They survived my Eighties *Fame* phase, when I wore leg warmers, big jumpers and belts and had my hair scrunched on top of my head like a giant pineapple; they said nothing when I dressed as Madonna, in a little black skirt, and ripped fishnets and adorned my arms with dozens of rubber bangles, which were actually Hoover parts that I had got from the DIY shop. It was only when I turned gothic that they made comments. I wore black from head to foot all the time and would spend hours piling on the dramatic black eye make-up, the white face powder and the dark lipstick. When I finally emerged from my room and came downstairs my mum would exclaim, 'Oh no, she's got her make-up on, don't say anything to upset her.' She'd observe that, as soon as I put my make-up on, I underwent a personality change and from being a lovely chatty girl I would mutate into a moody, monosyllabic teenager – think Harry Enfield's Kevin the Teenager and you won't be far off the mark. But she said it jokingly. She and Dad were happy for me to experiment and it's not as if

I was making myself look sexually provocative, clad in a long black dress and masked in hideous face paint.

Although at one time I had thought I wanted to be a fashion designer, I didn't really know what I wanted to do in life. I imagined that I would get married and have children and look after them. I did think about being an air hostess – for purely superficial reasons. I thought they always looked so glamorous in their uniforms and immaculate make-up (this was before my goth phase) and I loved the thought of all that travel! But I didn't really have a clue what to do when I finished my GSCEs. I definitely didn't want to do 'A' levels though, so I decided to go to college and study Business and Accountancy. Mum and Dad also persuaded me to take a secretarial course, saying that it would be a useful thing to fall back on. So I enrolled at North East Surrey College of Technology. After my fairly strict school it was great to have more freedom and to mix with boys!

A few months after the unfortunate time with my bit of rough I met my first 'proper' boyfriend. James was very handsome, with dark-blond hair (yes, I had a bit of thing about it back then), blue eyes and a stocky physique. He played football and I fancied him like crazy. We went on long romantic walks together in the park, hung out in the shopping centre and finally I decided that he was the 'one' I was going to lose my virginity to. I was sweet sixteen and frankly not particularly experienced, in spite of all the dates in Spudulike and all the slow dances, but I felt the time was right. It was a big deal for me, though, and as the Saturday night drew nearer I became increasingly nervous. Conveniently, James's parents were out for the night and he threw a party, during which he and I went upstairs to his bedroom to do the deed. I didn't tell him that I was still a virgin but he didn't have to be Einstein to work it out because there was blood everywhere. Honestly, all the books I had ever read mentioned that there might be a bit of blood, but this was like the Texas Chainsaw Massacre! I was mortified when I saw the state of his sheets. I would have felt better had I actually enjoyed the experience, but as it was I thought it was painful and not at all what it was cracked up to be.

It was the kiss of death for our fledgling relationship. We tried it a few more times and things improved marginally, but then I finished with him. In those days I went off boys pretty quickly – novelty was everything.

Someone who I didn't go off that quickly, though, was Aleco (the Greek version of Alex), a Greek Adonis I met on the annual family holiday to Corfu. He had his own water-sport company on the beach and I'd been infatuated with him since the age of thirteen, but as he was some six years older than me he had older fish to fry. However, when I turned fifteen he took a bit a shine to me and started flirting. I was in seventh heaven, making my little sister Jo wild with envy, especially when he asked my parents if he could take me out for dinner and they said yes. I sat in one of the many tavernas in Corfu town, thrilled to be with this incredibly handsome man. He had dark-brown hair and beautiful dark eyes and of course a beautiful toned, tanned body.

My parents were much too kind to point out that he probably had a different holiday romance every two weeks. Unlike my other romances, however, this one didn't fizzle out quickly and we wrote regularly to each other, both longing for the summer holidays. When I was seventeen he actually bought a set of matching rings for us, with 'Alex' inscribed in each. I thought it was a very sweet gesture. It was only when my parents' friends went out to Corfu and discovered he was telling everyone that he was engaged to me that the penny dropped. I had thought nothing of it because he wore the ring on his right hand – I didn't realise that this was the hand the Greeks wore their engagement rings on! Apparently I was engaged but I didn't know it!

It was a very short engagement. Much as I adored Aleco, I had no intention of moving to Corfu. Besides, I had just met someone else – someone who had swept me off my feet.

CHAPTER TWO

THE PREMIER LEAGUE

As soon as I set eyes on him in the summer of 1989, I was dazzled. Quite simply, John Scales was one of the best-looking men I had ever seen. He was six foot three, with an amazing physique, and with his classical good looks, blond hair and blue eyes, he looked like a young Robert Redford. He seemed way out of my league and I didn't imagine for a second that this 23-year-old footballer would be interested in a teenage college girl like me.

I had met him through my best friend Lucy because her older sister Emma was going out with – and later married – Alan Cork, one of John's teammates. As John had recently joined Wimbledon FC and didn't know anyone in London, Alan had taken him under his wing and introduced him to Emma's family and friends.

Both Lucy and me were completely besotted with John – whenever he turned up at Lucy's house our hearts would race and we would only have eyes for him. Not only was John blessed with stunning good looks, but he was also a charming and intelligent man. He was not at all a stereotypical footballer – barely able to string a sentence together, only interested in football, birds and cars. No, John was articulate and funny; really, this man had everything!

One hot summer's day Alan, John and Emma were going out for a drink in Cobham and to our delight they invited Lucy and me along. That day, luckily, I was wearing one of my favourite outfits – denim shorts that I had made myself by cutting up a pair of American Classic jeans, a black scoop-necked top with little white hearts on it and trainers; my shoulder-length blonde hair was highlighted and I was tanned. I think I looked good. And now I had reason to be glad I had spent so much time doing lengths in the pool, because my body was slim and toned. I've been fortunate in that I've never really had to struggle to stay slim and I've always been careful about what I eat. I don't eat potatoes, I try and avoid bread, though I do adore toast, and I actually don't like chocolate. (Please don't hate me! I have other hang-ups…)

John picked us up in his rather gorgeous motor – a sporty Peugeot GTI; it was a definite improvement to be driven in a car that hadn't been nicked! And it was certainly a flashier model than any of the boys I knew could hope to drive. Lucy and I sat in the back, thrilled to be so close to this gorgeous man. Suddenly I became aware that John was repeatedly staring at me in the mirror. I felt acutely self-conscious – partly excited by his interest and partly embarrassed – and kept looking away shyly.

We arrived at the pub, but I suffered a major disappointment when John's girlfriend turned up – someone who I didn't even know existed. I remember bitchily thinking that she was nothing special! I was also secretly pleased to see that they didn't really interact together. Emma told me it was very 'on off'. More 'off' please, I thought. I didn't stop to think that it was strange that he had a girlfriend and yet he was making eyes at me – I was far too young and too besotted at the time to realise what that might imply.

Even though his girlfriend was by his side, John kept staring at me. Now I was growing more confident and I stared back. He really was gorgeous and I longed for something to happen between us. But we were both shy and I was hardly likely to make the first move. Over the next few weeks there were several other occasions when we all went out as a group and all John and I did was sneak glances at each other, which only increased my longing for him.

Then, one night Emma had a request that set my heart racing – 'Alex, John wants your number, can I give it to him?' There's nothing in the world to match the agony of waiting for a phone call when you're that age. I suppose nowadays it would be a call on a mobile or a text, but back then I could only hover by the phone, praying for it to ring. I kept picking it up to check that it was working. Then, finally, it rang. Mum got there first. 'Alex,' she shouted to me, 'there's some-one called John on the phone for you.'

I came running down the stairs and grabbed the receiver from her, my throat suddenly dry, my stomach doing somersaults with nervousness.

'Hi,' John said, 'how are you?'

'Totally head over heels passionately in love with you.' I didn't say it, of course, but instead mumbled something about being fine.

We'd never really had a proper conversation before – it had all been in the eye contact – so I was very nervous to be talking to him at last. To my delight, though, he asked me out for dinner the following Saturday. He would pick me up after the match.

I was elated. My parents, on the other hand, were very tight-lipped. They hadn't met John and were convinced that he would be a brain-dead gigolo with a drug habit. I was oblivious to them, though, and spent the next week in a delicious state of anticipation. Saturday was a blisteringly hot day and I decided to lie in the garden to top up my tan. I had zero interest in football but decided I had better brush up my knowledge pretty sharpish, so I listened to the results on the radio. What a big yawn that was – really, I just couldn't see what the fuss was about! I was also very nervous and decided I needed some Dutch courage, so I cracked open the bottle of ouzo I'd brought back from my Greek holiday. It is foul stuff and to make it more drinkable I added lemonade. It was a fatal mistake: the hot weather had made me very thirsty and that, combined with the nerves, meant that before I knew it I had knocked back nearly half the bottle. By six o'clock I wasn't nervous any more – I was drunk. Fortunately, before I lost the plot completely I had at least decided on my outfit. Like any teenage girl I was always acutely conscious of what I looked like and had spent hours that week agonising over what to wear, trying on every single item of clothing I possessed. Even at that age I never wanted to look tarty, so I'd gone for denim jeans and a denim sleeveless shirt – a classic look, I thought. John obviously thought so too, because when Mum opened the door to him he was also wearing denim.

Like every other female who met him, Mum was instantly bowled over by John's good looks and charm. She admitted later that he was the total opposite of what she had imagined and she had no reservations as she waved me goodbye.

The night was a complete blur to me. At the restaurant I had a couple of glasses of wine and by then I was paralytic. I managed to get through the meal without disgracing myself, but it must have been obvious to John that I was hopelessly drunk. As he pulled up in my parents' drive we may have had a goodnight kiss – I really don't remember. What I *do* remember is falling out of the car and having to pick myself up and stagger into the house. I was mortified the next day, convinced that I would never see him again. But incredibly he called, and after teasing me about how drunk I had been he said he wanted to see me again.

We went on a few more dates and I managed to stay off the ouzo. Right from the start we were very attracted to each other. Within two months I had fallen in love with him and was spending all my free time with him. Soon, goodnight kisses weren't enough and we became lovers. This time round I *could* see what all the fuss was about. Sex could be pleasurable after all, not just something to be endured with gritted teeth! Actually, the sex with John was fantastic and a major part of our relationship. We couldn't get enough of each other. I lived for the times I could go round to his house and make love with him. In contrast to my previous boyfriends, John had his own place, so I didn't have to worry constantly that his parents would walk in at an inopportune moment, which was a relief. I found that I lost my inhibitions with him and we made love all over the house. We definitely didn't confine ourselves to the bedroom. The sexual chemistry between us was so strong that often when we were out clubbing we'd slip off to the Ladies for a quick one – naughty, I know, but very nice…

Initially it was everything I had ever dreamed a relationship could be – intense, passionate, physically and emotionally fulfilling. I loved him, he loved me; I was blissfully happy. The one slight downside was having to watch him play football every Saturday. The beautiful game leaves me cold, which is ironic, when you consider who I went on to marry. I definitely wasn't one of those ladettes who wanted to show off their knowledge of the offside rule. All I knew was that there were two goalposts at either end of the pitch and that at half-time the teams changed sides – and even that took a bit of getting used to! By the end of the match I'd have read the programme from cover to cover, anything to avoid looking at the game, and if I could I would try and stay in the players' lounge after half-time and have a gossip with some of the other girlfriends. Inevitably, if I did that it would be one of the times John would score, even though he wasn't a striker. 'Did you see my goal?' he would demand after the game.

'Well,' I'd reply, 'not exactly.'

He'd raise his eyebrows and say, 'Were you in the lounge again?' But I don't think he minded that I was a football dunce. He spent his entire week playing the game, and I think the last thing he wanted was to talk tactics to me.

There were definite pressures attached to going out with a top-league player, mainly over what you looked like. The other footballers' wives and girlfriends really did get dressed up for a game and tried to outdo each other in the glamour stakes, and I felt obliged to look my best. I would end up having to plan my wardrobe the week before, and casual was definitely out. I took to wearing smart designer suits, or leather trousers, high-heeled boots and jackets. I had to look groomed and immaculate, with perfect make-up, a tan and my long blonde hair blow-dried straight. Only once did I make a fashion faux pas. I was late arriving at the stands and as I made my way down the steps I could see

John looking at me in disbelief. As soon as we met up in the players' lounge he said, 'You can't come to a match in shorts!' I tried to explain that they weren't shorts, but culottes and actually the height of fashion for that week, but he was having none of it.

It wasn't just the footballers' wives who made me want to look my best, though. Whenever I went out with John he was like a babe magnet. Women would stare at him shamelessly and often start chatting him up, even when I was with him. I was constantly having to look over my shoulder to check out the opposition.

Saturdays after the match were always big social events and we would invariably go out for dinner with the other players and their partners, then go on to a nightclub. We both enjoyed going out and socialising, but we liked being on our own together more. We'd go out for dinner, long walks or indulge in our passion for shopping – in fact, John was even more into buying clothes than I was, which is saying something. We were also quite sporty together and went go-karting and quad-biking.

We even went windsurfing. John was one of those sickening people who are good at everything they try – he was great at rugby and golf too – but for once I was looking forward to showing off my superior technique. I'd tried windsurfing on one of my Greek holidays and was sure I would be better than John. But, typically, John was brilliant as soon as he got on the board, whereas I spent most of the sessions stuck on an island. On Wednesdays he only trained in the morning, so I would skive from college to spend the rest of the day with him. I'm afraid my college work did suffer slightly as a result.

John and I were intensely close and I wanted to be with him all the time, but looking back I think it was unhealthy. We were in our own little world, but it was a world where he definitely held the upper hand. I was so smitten that at first I didn't really see what a commitment-phobe he was – and, besides, I was hardly expecting to move in with him straight away. But two years into our relationship he was still holding on to his space and telling me that we really shouldn't live together yet. Yes, I could stay round his house – and by now he lived down the road from me in Cheam – but I was living out of carrier bags. I could never leave any of my clothes there, not even a spare pair of pants. He made a major concession when he let me keep a toothbrush there but, if ever his sister, who was very religious, came to stay, it would be hidden away. He also hated having his picture taken and refused to have any photographs taken with me – it was as if a photograph would prove that he was in a relationship and he could no longer pretend that it wasn't serious.

As for going on holiday, well, in five years we only went away once together: a week in the Lake District, camping with some friends. It was very pleasant, but bearing in mind he was a professional footballer, he really could have treated us to a trip to Barbados! We camped in a field full of sheep and shared a tent with one of his friends and his girlfriend, which obviously put paid to any romantic activities. If we wanted to get up to anything we would have to sneak into the woods and make love alfresco – which is all very Lady Chatterley, but also quite chilly and indeed at times painful if you happened to lie back in patch of nettles, as I managed to. We completed the outdoor sexathon by skinny-dipping in a freezing cold river and I had a momentary pang for the warm seas of the Caribbean as I watched my body turn blue. I couldn't even have a hot shower, as there was only a sink at the local farmhouse. I suppose I thought that one day things would be different and we would eventually go abroad together.

John was a pretty generous boyfriend, but I wouldn't exactly say that he lavished presents on me; I often felt I had to work for them! His generosity tended to come out at birthdays and Christmas. For my eighteenth birthday he bought me a lovely bracelet made out of three types of gold, and for my nineteenth he bought me a golden retriever puppy – mind you, that was only on the condition that it was half his, and was to be called Seve, after his favourite golfer. John usually had impeccable taste when it came to buying me things and once bought me a set of beautiful underwear from La Perla. But his good taste deserted him on our second Christmas together. I had been dropping heavy hints about wanting a black leather biker's jacket for Christmas; I really don't think I could have made my desires any clearer. But come Christmas Day I ripped open the large parcel to discover a perfectly hideous designer jacket. Put it this way: a sixty-year-old would have looked quite good in it, but not an eighteen-year-old. It was grey cashmere with a belt and had a big Native American Indian embroidered on the back. I looked a fright, a complete frump. I spent the day giggling hysterically on the sofa with my best friend Julie – her boyfriend had bought her a horrible ring – while the men looked at us in total bemusement.

In July 1990 I left college with my BTEC diplomas in Business and Accountancy. I still wasn't sure what I wanted to do and decided I would take the rest of the summer off and generally laze around. I thought I might get some modelling work – I had already some bits and pieces, mainly appearing in the photo love stories in comics such as *Jackie* and *My Guy*. One storyline, which ran for five weeks, was about a couple of teenagers who used to meet up secretly by a beautiful old tree, which then got destroyed in the big storm in the Eighties. I think the young lovers' romance might have petered out after that; it probably wasn't the same meeting by a stump! I became very good at looking lovestruck and moody – mind you, as a teenager myself I didn't exactly have to work hard at it. I'd also modelled for some topless calendars – not an experience I particularly enjoyed. When I married George I was expecting the pictures to come back and haunt me, but they finally emerged only when I appeared in *I'm A Celebrity...* My body looked OK, it was my big Eighties hairdo that was the real shocker!

John was appalled when he found out that I was planning to be a slacker for the whole summer. He had a very strong work ethic and managed to make me feel guilty. So I ended up going to interviews, to show a bit of willing. One of them was with a company which was owned and run by an entrepreneur photographer. As well as photography, they did film shoots and adverts; they also had a graphics department and made and sold exhibition stands. The company had a great feel about it and I loved the fact that there was so much going on, so when they offered me the job of receptionist I took it.

For a good few months I loved it. I really enjoyed meeting all the different people who turned up at the studio and there was never a dull moment. I also liked working in the heart of London – the studio was in Covent Garden, so it was great for socialising after work. However, it was an American company and they wanted to squeeze as much work out of us as possible – I would have to be in from breakfast, and if I left any earlier than six I would be treated as if I was skiving! Because I was the junior, I ended up having to do everything and I rapidly became shattered and rather fed up.

Eventually I moved on to another job in the same company as PA to one of the directors, but I hated it. My boss wasn't particularly pleasant and it made me miserable working for someone who never had a good word to say to anybody. Also, I was becoming increasingly tired of being stuck in an office. It would have been bearable if things between John and me were going well, but as it was he was about to deliver a bombshell.

For two years we had been intensely close, totally in love with each other, and, while he studiously avoided talking about the future, by now I couldn't imagine mine without him – he was everything to me. In the summer of 1991 he promised to come on holiday with my parents and me. I couldn't wait; it seemed like a major breakthrough. Next time, I imagined that we would be able to go off on our own. Then he called me from Yorkshire, where he would always go during the summer when he wasn't playing.

'I'm sorry, I can't see you any more.' His voice sounded cold and detached.

I was totally stunned. 'Why not?' I asked.

'I'm sorry, I just don't want to be with you any more.'

I felt as if my world was ending. But I didn't cry, I didn't beg. I somehow managed to say, 'Fine', and put the phone down. Only then did I cry. I was absolutely heartbroken by his rejection. I couldn't believe that he wanted to end our relationship. I couldn't imagine what had changed. There had been no warning signs: we didn't argue, he hadn't stopped saying that he loved me, the sex was better than ever – so what the hell was going on?

I was too proud and too stubborn to call him. And I couldn't forgive him for ending things by phone. It seemed a particularly heartless thing to do. Looking back, though, I suppose I was lucky – no doubt if mobile phones had been around he would have dumped me by text.

I can only imagine that he thought we were getting too serious and, even though I knew he loved me, he couldn't bear to commit to a long-term relationship. I went away as planned with my mum and dad, trying to put on a brave face and make the best of things, but I was so hurt. I was nineteen and I had lost what I thought was the love of my life. I don't think I had known pain like it. I thought I would never recover.

Back from holiday, I still held back from calling him. I carried on pretending that everything was fine, but inside I was a mess. I even ended up going out with someone on the rebound. Before I had split with John we had spent quite a lot of time at the local Surrey cricket club and Andy – one of the cricketers, a very good-looking guy – had paid me a lot of attention. Whenever we went to the club I would be aware of him watching me, but I didn't think anything of it because I was with John. He had even got hold of my work number and would often call me. Now I was single, things were different and I ended up going out on a few dates with him. I suppose I thought that if I saw someone else it would help me get over John. But actually it just made me miss him even more. Andy was a perfectly nice guy, attractive and sexy, but he just didn't do it for me. After he had taken me for dinner one night we ended up at his house. I knew what was on the cards when he kissed me. Part of me wanted to leave; part of me said, 'Oh you may as well.' So we had sex in the lounge. It was a total rebound shag, deeply unsatisfying and awkward – his parents were asleep upstairs. Afterwards, I felt empty. Who was I kidding? I didn't want anyone else. I wanted John.

Despite feeling so blue, I did manage to get another job – at the time, any change felt like it had to be for the better. I left Academy and became a sales rep for a company that specialised in printing and reprographics, art design and exhibition stands. They also sold stationery, and on my first day I found myself in possession of a Vauxhall Cavalier and a large stationery catalogue and I was told to go off and make some sales. I hadn't been given any training and didn't have a clue about any of the products.

I sat in a little café in Richmond, flicking through the catalogue and feeling rather daunted. John Bird, the founder of *The Big Issue*, was also in there and he got chatting to me, telling me all about the new charity for the homeless he had just set up. When he found out what I did, he immediately told me that I should come over to his new office, as they hadn't yet got any stationery. I ended up taking a major order from him and my boss was delighted. I was the golden girl.

I did enjoy my new job. I liked being out and about and, even though cold-calling could be nerve-racking, I tried to detach myself and not take it too personally when I got turned away. I became firm friends with Julie, another sales rep, and we would meet up for lunch – a sure way of making up for a bad sales morning. She went on to become one of my closest friends, and she still is today.

Despite the buzz I got from my new job, I still desperately missed John. I didn't want to be surrounded by anything that reminded me of him, so next I ended up selling my car. It was a jeep and I think everyone thought that he had bought it for me, though he hadn't. He was never that generous! He'd simply helped me get the loan for it and had been there when I bought it.

I hadn't seen or spoken to John for nearly three months. To try and distract myself and avoid brooding over him I went on holiday to Gran Canaria with a friend. It was my one and only 18–30 holiday and I can honestly say that I hated every minute of it. I spent the week drinking myself into oblivion and being pursued by lecherous Essex boys. The only good thing to come of it was that I found out on my return that John had discovered I had been seeing Andy and was furious and very jealous. He also thought that I had gone away with Andy, and was apparently gutted. I heard from one of his teammates that the Wimbledon manager, Joe Kinnear, had had a quiet word with the team when John wasn't around, telling them, 'Can't you lot do something to get him back with Alex? I can't do anything with him while he's moping around like this.' I also found out from a friend that John had called me at my old work number, and I hoped it had given him pause for thought when he discovered that I had left. It was my way of saying I had moved on, that I could get on without him, even though I didn't feel that way inside.

Finally I got the call I had longed for. After asking me

how I was, John asked if we could get back together. I didn't hesitate, I said yes straight away. I didn't tell him how much he had hurt me and he made no apology for having dumped me so unceremoniously. Over dinner he admitted that he was scared of commitment. He said that he thought he was too young to have a serious relationship and too young to get married. There was no big declaration that he loved me; he was just expecting us to carry on as before. I said that was fine by me, that I was also too young for a serious relationship. But I didn't mean it. At the time I wanted him back at any price. So we got back together, but exclusively on his terms. Yes, he wanted to be with me, but he wasn't going to commit. I thought I might as well settle for that, rather than be totally heartbroken.

John had changed since we had split up, though. During that time he had moved into Wimbledon village, acquired a new circle of friends and bought himself a flashy, bright-blue Porsche. Suddenly the modest, down-to-earth man I knew was no longer recognisable. He was becoming more successful as a player, and other clubs were showing an interest in him. He had never seemed that bothered by the attention other women paid him when we went out, but now he seemed to revel in it. His teammates started to call him 'Gigolo' – unfortunately, it took me a while to cotton on to the full significance of that nickname.

For the next three years I was put through the emotional wringer. I loved John and because of that I put up with his lack of commitment. Now I wonder why on earth I did, but I was young and naïve – I would rather be with him, even if at times he did treat me badly, than be on my own, or with anyone else. He was my first big love and that's not an easy thing to walk away from. That summer set the pattern for our relationship – we'd be together for six months or so and then he would decide that he needed a break, that he wanted more 'space'. God, how I came to hate that word! We wouldn't see each other for two months, during which time I would be miserable, heartbroken and longing to see him, and then he would call and we'd get back together. The sexual attraction between us was very strong, and however much he hurt me I always wanted him. The reconciliations after the break-ups would always be passionate and addictive – when I was lying in his arms I would forget about all those nights when I cried myself to sleep.

Every time he said he wanted a break I felt another piece of my heart splinter, but I never crumbled in front of him, I never begged him to take me back. I picked myself up and got on with my life. The first time he rejected me I had learned a hard and valuable lesson: not to ditch my friends for any man. I had spent so much time with John that I drifted away from my friends and I had to make a real effort to get back in touch with them. I promised myself that it wouldn't happen again.

In October 1992, when I was 20, I fell pregnant. I only realised when I had a miscarriage. I woke up one morning in agony; I was bleeding heavily and had severe stomach cramps. When I went to the doctor he told me I was miscarrying; I had been two months pregnant. I found the whole experience very upsetting, even more so when I told John. He did not seem able to give me the sympathy I needed, but wanted to know how it had happened, as if this was something I had deliberately set out to do, and muttered that we 'needed to be more careful in future'. I desperately wanted him to show me some love and reassurance – not only was I in physical pain, I also felt a real sense of loss. I had always wanted to have children and, even though my relationship with John was rocky, I would have had this baby. I had to have an operation in hospital and I felt utterly wretched. Afterwards I went to Derbyshire to stay with an uncle. I needed time to recover and I needed to be far away from John. I felt very let down by him.

That probably should have been my wake-up call to leave this man once and for all. I might have kidded myself that I was strong enough to deal with his rejection but I'm sure it wasn't good for me. It seemed as if we were hell bent on acting out that cliché – we couldn't live with each other and we couldn't live without each other. But John made it harder and harder. He started saying that he couldn't see me at the weekends because he wanted to go out with his friends. I put on my inevitable brave face and made sure that I went out with my friends – I wasn't going to sit at home and mope. The trouble was, when I went out all I saw were men who couldn't compare with

John. I couldn't break the hold he had over me. Even after the miscarriage, I didn't want to. And, even when I began to suspect that he might be seeing other women, I still couldn't.

We'd just ended up in bed together after one of our 'mini break-ups'. John had gone to have a bath, but I felt unable to relax. Then I noticed a card with a teddy bear on it lying blatantly on the chest of drawers. I opened it. Inside, someone – some woman – had written: 'Thanks for another lovely weekend.' You bloody bastard, I thought. Is this why you never see me at the weekends any more? I stormed into the bathroom, waving the card in his face.

'What's this?' I demanded.

He shrugged and tried to look unconcerned. 'It's just a woman I met. I only saw her because I didn't know what was happening with us. It was nothing serious.'

But that wasn't all. I started to feel as if I couldn't trust him. One time he was away on tour and I let myself into his house. I felt terrible rifling through his things, but I couldn't stop myself. I found several pieces of paper with phone numbers on them. I stuffed them in my pocket and was about to leave when I noticed a letter that had just been delivered. I carefully prised it open. It was from a friend of ours and I couldn't believe what I was reading! He had enclosed a picture of his very pretty stepdaughter, along with the words, 'I know you like a change sometimes.' The cheek of it! I rushed home with my hoard. I burned the letter and the picture and then I set about phoning those numbers to see who answered. They were all women and when I checked the area codes I found out that they all lived in areas where John had been touring. Of course, the numbers didn't mean that he had been unfaithful, but it wasn't very nice knowing that your boyfriend had kept them as if saving them up for a rainy day. I often got chatted up but never dreamed of giving anyone my number or taking theirs. John was all I wanted, but it seemed I wasn't enough for him.

In retrospect, perhaps it wasn't so surprising – after all, women were constantly eyeing him up or chatting him up. One incident, which happened on my 21st birthday, is burned into my memory. John had very generously given me £400 to go and buy myself a set of rings I had fallen in love with and I'd had a great party with a friend of ours who shared a birthday with me. We'd had a fairly wild night, dancing and drinking, and everyone had ended up staying at the house. I had crashed out in bed in the early hours with John and his friend Robbie – to sleep I hasten to add, nothing more. I woke up suddenly to discover that one of the women at the party – who was married, with a baby – had crept into bed with us and was caressing John's body and actually kissing his nipples! John wasn't telling her to stop.

I woke Robbie up. 'Look what's going on,' I hissed, but he was so out of it he just mumbled, 'Go back to sleep.' Nothing was further from my mind. I grabbed the woman's arm. 'Excuse me,' I snapped, 'that's my boyfriend!' She made a sharp exit. Yes, that's right, I thought furiously, you get back to your husband and baby and leave my man alone!

When I challenged John about it later that day, he claimed he couldn't remember. If this is what happened when I was there, God only knows what happened when I wasn't!

Several other things happened that made me start to re-evaluate my relationship. A group of us had gone back to a friend's house after having dinner. We'd all had a few drinks and were quite merry. Then John disappeared into the kitchen for what seemed like ages. Knowing full well he wouldn't be doing the washing up, I went to see what he was up to. I walked in and discovered him snogging the teenaged daughter of one of our friends!

'That's it!' I shouted, 'You bastard, I'm leaving!' I really thought I meant it that time – but apparently not. I carried on my on-off relationship with him for the rest of that year, which culminated in one last humiliation. I went with him to Wimbledon FC's Christmas party, and he completely ignored me, preferring to spend the night chatting up some women he knew from his gym. Now I knew exactly why he was called 'Gigolo'.

I decided I needed to make a major change in my life and break my dependency on John. When I was at school I had thought about becoming an air hostess and now I seriously started to consider it. I'd had enough of my sales rep job. I had done really well at it, became one of the top reps in the country and was earning quite a bit of commission, but I'd stopped getting a buzz

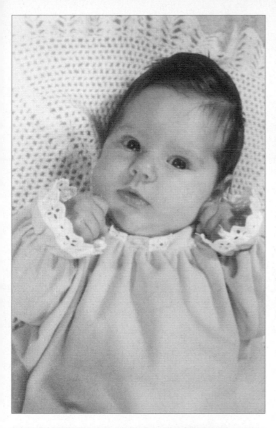

Alexandra Macadam Pursey makes her entrance into the world.

Above left: At six weeks old.

Above right: Saddle up! My first Christmas.

Below left: Learning to smile for the camera from a young age.

Below right: On holiday in Portugal, pictured here with Mum and my sister Jo.

My beautiful mum –
this was the picture
that was taken when
she applied to become
an air hostess – like
mother, like daughter.

Mum and Dad, who have been there for me no matter what.

Above: Dad looking sharp and Mum looking glam at a dinner in 1966.

Below: Wedding bells were ringing in May 1969.

Sisterly love – Jo and I have always been close.

Above left: Perhaps Jo was unhappy with my driving?

Above right: Displaying the latest in towelling fashions – all the rage in the seventies.

Below left: I had a serious flick to take with me to primary school that day.

Below right: Jo and I with my first pony, Bamber.

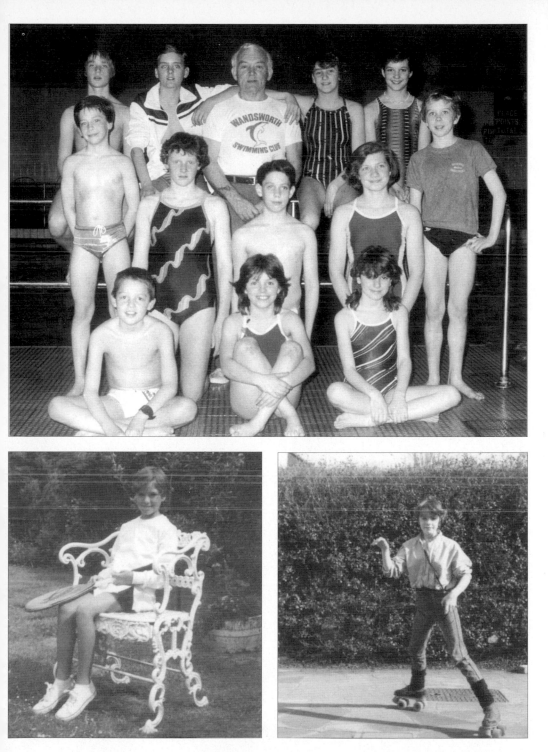

I loved sports when I was a girl, though these hobbies were eventually given up in favour of socialising and boys!

Above: The Wandsworth Dolphins swimming club – that's me, front row, far right.

Below left: Anyone for tennis?

Below right: Rollergirl at the ready.

Above: My first day at Greenacre in September 1983 – the uniform was later customised to suit my tastes!

Below: Getting stuck into my homework.

Hold on to your sun hats, the girls are on holiday …

Above: In Greece – I'm in the middle, wearing sunglasses – Jo is at the front of the boat, Heidi's to the left of me and Lucy to the right.

Below left: With Lucy in Spain.

Below right: The days when big hair was the order of the day. In Corfu with Heidi.

Above: On the annual family holiday in Corfu, where I met the Greek Adonis!

Below: On holiday in France, 17 years old.

from it and my boss was really starting to be on my case. I'm not sure if he resented my success because I was a woman, but he began checking up on me all the time. One day I was out of my area, on my way to have lunch with Julie, when I shouldn't have been. Out of the blue, my boss called me and asked me where I was. I lied and said I was in Twickenham, about to make a call. He replied, 'That's funny because there's a girl driving along the embankment in front of me in a car with exactly the same registration number as yours, talking on the phone.' I looked in my mirror and, sure enough, there he was. I ended up getting a written warning and they piled the work on, demanding constant reports from me. I really resented it, thinking, I've brought in all this new business for you, how dare you treat me like this! So one evening when I was out with a friend having a drink and my boss called wanting a report from me first thing in the morning, I told him where he could stick his job. Then I went home and typed up my resignation letter. I didn't care. I already had a job lined up at Virgin.

CHAPTER THREE

FLYING HIGH

'Excuse me, Miss, do you think you could store this for me please?'

'Of course, Sir,' I replied, flashing the passenger my most sincere air-hostess smile and trying not to dissolve into giggles as he handed me his artificial leg, complete with shoe and sock. As I walked the length of the plane holding the leg in my arms I couldn't help thinking that this wasn't exactly what I had imagined when I joined Virgin!

I'd always wanted to travel, so a job that paid me to do just that was my dream ticket. I definitely didn't want to back-pack and slum it in hostels. A luxury hotel was much more up my street and with Virgin I would get to stay in five-star hotels. I faced stiff competition to get a place in the airline. It had not been established for very long, and there was definite kudos and glamour associated with the brand. This wasn't some budget operation – people flew with Virgin because they wanted to travel in style and they expected the air hostesses to be a cut above the others.

I was thrilled when I found out I had got the job, in January 1994. The news was followed by an intensive training course. People often dismiss air hostesses as trolley dollies, just there to look pretty and act as glorified waitresses, but they should try doing it! The training was physically and mentally gruelling; we had to learn the SEP manual – Safety and Emergency Procedures – off by heart. Even when we started flying, we had to reel it off before every flight and every eight months you were tested on it. If you failed, you were out. Every day on our training course we had a test and we had to achieve at least 80 per cent. I also had to be able to administer first aid, go into an aircraft that was on fire and jump out using the emergency slides, and all without batting an eyelid.

I have to make a girly admission here – I adored my uniform. It was designed by the Emmanuels, and I thought it was stunning. It was a scarlet suit, with a tight pencil skirt and a classic eighties power jacket, a smart cream shirt and bright red stilettos. We actually had to have lessons on how to apply our make-up and how to put our hair up. And once we were flying we had frequent grooming checks: your lipstick had to be exactly the right shade of red, nails had to be varnished in red or clear polish and you were reprimanded if you weren't wearing enough make-up! It was exactly the opposite of my school days, when I was forever being ordered to wash off the slap.

Six long weeks later, I passed. To celebrate our success, we were given a lunch and Sir Richard Branson was there to hand out our certificates and our 'wings'. I waited patiently for him to call out my name, but he missed me out! Apparently he always does this to one person; typically, it had to be me. I put up my hand and called out, 'Excuse me!' at which point he laughed and presented me with my wings.

Then I was off. My first flight was to Miami, and I loved the whole experience. I loved being down route even more. It was February and back in England it was raining; meanwhile I was sunning myself on the beach. My other routes included San Francisco and Los Angeles. Best of all I would get to stay in these cities for four nights – even when I flew to New York I would stay for two nights. We were given an allowance of $109 a night while we were away, on top of our salary – just as well, as I had taken a massive pay cut and now earned seven grand a year!

It was just like being on an extended holiday once you were down route. I'd be with a fantastic group of girls; we were all the same age and all up for a laugh. We stayed in gorgeous hotels, lazed on the beach or by the pool, went shopping, went out clubbing and we were getting paid for it – this was definitely my kind of job. And when I wasn't flying I sometimes got modelling jobs, which helped boost my income. I'd model for the Clothes Show in Birmingham, or be one of the models at the Boat Show, which simply involved posing on a boat in a bikini – not exactly taxing, then!

Other jobs required slightly more effort but there was always a way round… on one occasion I had to hand out promotional leaflets on a busy high street. It was very tedious and the more leaflets we got rid of, the more the organisers gave us. Eventually, one of the other girls said she'd had enough and she led me to an enormous skip at the end of the road. Once there we dumped our leaflets – and I noticed that the skip was already full of leaflets from other companies!

Of course, the downside to flying was the jet lag, which could be crippling. That, and some of the passengers, who could be totally obnoxious. On one flight a woman kept pressing her call buzzer and demanding things without a word of please or thanks. Finally I snapped when she once more called me over and said, 'Coke.'

'And?' I asked her, meaning a please would be nice, but she just said 'Coke' again. Right, I thought, if you want Coke you can have it. So I went to the galley, took a can from the fridge and shook it violently. Then I handed it to her with a smile and beat a hasty retreat, watching from a distance as she opened the can and the Coke exploded over her. Of course, she called me back in a rage. 'I'm very sorry,' I replied sweetly, 'but we've experienced some turbulence.' Not.

Some male passengers could be rather lecherous, but I just smiled politely and made it clear I wasn't interested – and anyway, even if you did meet a man who seemed nice, we were strictly forbidden to hand out our phone numbers to passengers. The other thing I am always asked is if I ever witnessed any 'mile-high' activities. Thankfully not – I really can't see the attraction of having sex in the toilets of a plane as even the ones in business class are tiny.

Getting my new job definitely helped me have a better perspective on my relationship with John. I was sick of being messed around by him, never knowing where I stood, whether today would be the one where he would say he needed a break. It was so bad for my self-esteem. We even ended up in the papers at the beginning of 1994, which I hated, though frankly it was nothing compared to what happened when I met George. John and I were out in Wimbledon with his teammates after a match, when he received a call from his agent, Eric Hall. I could tell there was something wrong by the look on his face and he went outside to carry on the conversation. When he returned, he took me to one side so we couldn't be overheard.

'Alex, I think you should know that it's going to come out in the press tomorrow that I've been seeing Britt Ekland.'

'What!' I exclaimed. 'Have you?'

'Of course not,' he said and then went on to explain that he had met her after a match and they had chatted, but that was it. In the past I probably would have accepted his explanation but I was fed up of his womanising reputation and I stormed out of the bar.

The following day the story of their alleged liaison

appeared in a tabloid. Both she and John denied that there was any truth in the rumour, but when I spoke to John on the phone he seemed rather pleased with himself. He appeared to enjoy the attention from the press. Then, of course, I had the press calling me trying to find out how I felt about it. I said nothing. Luckily, a few days later I flew to the States for a holiday with a girlfriend and I was able to escape the press madness.

When I returned, inevitably I saw John again. I couldn't seem to break the connection between us. The physical attraction I still felt for him overruled my better judgement, but I was toughening up emotionally. Now if he messed me around I knew I could just get on a plane, go somewhere lovely and have a good time with my friends. Somehow, being the one who was away made me less concerned about what he was up to. He, on the other hand, hated my new job. I think for the first time in our relationship the balance of power seemed to be shifting and now he was left wondering what I was doing. Also, I would see him on my terms – it would be me calling him, saying that I was back from a flight. He had to accept that I wasn't available all the time at his beck and call.

By the summer of 1994, our relationship was on a definite downward spiral. I'd had enough of being picked up and put down when he felt like it. Increasingly we seemed to be leading separate lives and it was getting harder to hold on to a dream that this might change one day – that one day his fear of commitment might end and he would ask me to marry him. I was finally able to end it at the beginning of July. By now we really weren't getting on at all well and I think I was psyching myself up to leave.

One night we were out at a small bar in Wimbledon with a group of friends. A rather attractive man came up to me and started chatting me up and, instead of doing what I would normally do and ignoring him, I responded. I wasn't really interested in him, I think I was just out to provoke John. When the man asked me for my phone number, I gave it to him. This was all in front of John and he went mad, shouting how dare I give another man my phone number!

I shrugged. 'I think that's it, don't you?' And it really was. We had split up and got back together so many times I had run out of emotion, I had nothing left to give this relationship. I knew if I stayed any longer nothing would ever change, it would be more of the same. And I didn't want to be with someone who couldn't commit. I wanted to be with someone who wasn't afraid to say they loved me. I wanted someone who wanted me one hundred per cent.

I was prepared to hold out for this if necessary, but incredibly I was to find it only two weeks later …

CHAPTER FOUR
BRIEF ENCOUNTER

It was such an enormous relief when I finally split up with John. At last, I told myself, I'm free: I can get on with my life, and stop obsessing over what he was doing and who he was seeing. I had spent the last three years on an emotional roller coaster, never knowing where I stood, never knowing if I was going to be pushed away yet again so he could have his 'space'. Enough! Now I was determined to enjoy my newly single state to the full. I told myself I had absolutely no intention of having a relationship for a very long time.

It didn't seem to be a sentiment that John shared. We'd only officially broken up for two weeks when I walked in to Browns in Covent Garden – somewhere that I had always seen as 'my place' – only to be confronted by the sight of John with his new girlfriend. He obviously didn't believe in letting the grass grow under his feet! I made a quick exit. While I was relieved that we were no longer together, I didn't need my nose rubbed in it.

So one hot Saturday night in July 1994, I set myself on a mission to have a good time. If John could move on so easily, then so could I. I'd arranged to meet my friend Trudie at one of my favourite London haunts – Quaglino's in Piccadilly. I loved the buzz of the upstairs bar; there was always a sophisticated clientele and, even better, there were always plenty of men prepared to buy attractive girls drinks! I was chilling out, enjoying the gossip and the wine, when my friend dropped a bombshell.

'Alex, there's something I think you should know. I hope you won't be too upset.' She went on to tell me about one of John's conquests I hadn't known about – an acquaintance of mine. Apparently, they had been seeing each other when John and I were supposed to be an item. Wasn't it enough that he already had a new girlfriend?

'Bloody bastard!' I exploded, startling the men hovering near us. Trudie looked at me with concern. I sighed and took a large sip of wine. 'It's OK,' I said. 'It's over. Thank God.' And I really meant it.

We got talking to a couple of men, perfectly nice, but not my types. They invited us along to Tramp, an exclusive members-only club in Jermyn Street and a celeb haunt where all the A-list stars used to go. In those days, men – even if they were members – could only get in if they took a woman. Hence our invitation. We agreed to go with them, knowing that once we were in we'd go our own way.

'Oh look, there's Johnny and George,' said Trudie as we walked into the bar at Tramp. 'I must say hello.' Johnny being Johnny Gold, the owner of Tramp, and George being George Best – one of the world's greatest ever footballers, famous drunk and legendary womaniser.

George and I smiled at each other as we were introduced. Of course, I knew who he was – you'd have to have been living under a stone not to – but I didn't really know much about him, which was hardly surprising, seeing as he retired from football the year I was born! I hadn't seen his infamous television interview on *Wogan* when he was so hopelessly drunk that when Terry asked what he did with himself these days he could only repeatedly reply that he liked 'screwing'.

I found myself sitting next to him and we immediately hit it off. I certainly wasn't fazed at meeting someone so famous. I found him incredibly easy to talk to, very good company and extremely flirtatious! But I loved the attention. Compliments from John had been thin on the ground in the final death throes of our relationship, and as I was still smarting from the news that my ex already had a new girlfriend it was wonderful hearing how beautiful I was from this charming, charismatic man. I was, though I didn't realise it then, exactly the type that George would go for, being young, tanned and blonde! At one point he really made me smile when he said that my top was too revealing. I had gone for a boho-chic look that night and was wearing a pretty brown silk skirt and a matching top with a laced-up bodice, which only gave a hint of cleavage – I'm not a put-it-all-out-there kind of girl.

There was a definite spark of attraction between us. I thought he had the most wonderful eyes I had ever seen – incredibly blue and sparkling. I didn't know then just how much older than me he was, but thought he looked pretty good, with his handsome, expressive face and dark hair that was only slightly greying. And he made it perfectly clear that he was very interested in me. But it was the conversation that really captivated me – he was so interested in finding out all about me and had so many fascinating stories of his own. We compared our experiences of the States – George having spent quite a few years in LA playing football and owning a bar, me having spent a lot of time in LA as it was one of my flying routes. The rest of the table carried on without us; we were in our own little world.

As the night ended, with all of us a little the worse for wear, he asked me for my phone number. I didn't have a pen to write it down and laughingly said he would never remember it. He insisted that he would, so I told him, convinced that he would forget it. As we shared a lift to our various homes George suddenly demanded to be dropped off at another club, where he said he had to collect a keyring a 'lady of the night' had stolen! Even in my slightly inebriated state this seemed a bizarre moment. Who was this 'lady', I wondered, and what was his connection with her? Maybe a few alarm bells should have been going off in my head at this point, but I let him kiss me goodnight and I sank back in the car seat and watched London go by through the window, smiling to myself and thinking, I've just met George Best!

The next morning George was true to his word and called me, saying that he wanted to see me again and asked if I would meet him for a drink. I agreed but as soon as I put the phone down, in the cold light of day and slightly hungover, I felt uncertain about whether I should go or not. I had really enjoyed his company and the flirtation, but I couldn't help thinking that he was rather old – a whopping 48 to my 22. What would my parents think? Well, actually I knew what they would think: they'd be horrified! George was the same age as my mum and only two years younger than my dad. Then I thought back over the night. I'd had a really good time with him. I decided to go and see him, figuring I had absolutely nothing to lose.

So I drove to Chelsea, where he lived. I remember thinking that we'd be meeting in some classy bar, full of beautiful people, as Chelsea is so up-market, and had dressed accordingly, in a very pretty black polka-dot summer dress. But the reality couldn't have been more different. George had invited me to his local pub, The Phene Arms, and we're not talking sophisticated gastro pub here. It was a very old, traditional London pub, tucked away off the King's Road, and had been there forever – well, since eighteen-something. As I walked in I don't know what shocked me most, the hideous flocked wallpaper and luridly patterned sticky carpet or the tables of very old men. There were even a few

Chelsea Pensioners having a quiet drink – that's how happening it was! It was like that moment in the film *An American Werewolf In London* where the characters walk into The Slaughtered Lamb and everyone in there stops what they are doing and simply stares at the strangers, as if they have arrived from another planet.

Bloody hell, I thought to myself, what a dive. George was sitting at what I would later discover was his table, with an enormous glass of white wine in front of him. I say glass, but it was actually more like a goldfish bowl. He was very pleased to see me and I'd have to say, even given the location, I was pleased to see him again. Immediately we picked up where we had left off the night before. The conversation flowed so easily between us, I couldn't believe that I had only just met him. He definitely had the gift of the gab and that, along with those blue eyes, was quite a devastating combination.

In fact, it was all going very smoothly when all of a sudden somebody in the bar mentioned Mary, in a way that made me think she and George were together. I asked George who she was and he admitted that she was his girlfriend but that the relationship was on the rocks and they weren't getting on well. Maybe I should have questioned him more closely, but I was caught up in the moment, enjoying his company and the flirtation too much. Also, George was extremely convincing in his explanation. I trusted him when he said that she was his business manager now and that that was all there was to their relationship.

After George had downed his wine (and that's exactly what he did – he didn't touch it for ages, then drank the lot in one go) and I had finished my regular-size glass of wine, he suggested we go and eat. 'Good idea,' I said, eager to get out of the pub and away from the scrutiny of the regulars. George suggested we go to a little place he knew in Shepherd's Market and on the drive there he raved about how delicious the food was. I was hoping the venue would prove a little more sophisticated than the pub, so I was somewhat taken aback when I discovered our destination was a baked-potato café! Sure, the baked potato and cheese I had was very nice, but hardly the haute cuisine I had been anticipating!

It didn't matter, though. I was enjoying being with him and it seemed a perfect way to spend a Sunday afternoon. He kept showering me with compliments, telling me how gorgeous I was, and I felt a little ping of excitement every time he touched my hand.

After lunch it was off somewhere else – another private members' club owned by Johnny Gold. George was known by everyone there and they all seemed very protective of him. I remember thinking, God, he really does drink a lot, as he downed yet more white wine. But he was a charming drunk, sweet and funny, and I was finding him very attractive. He was the typical loveable rogue – you know you should steer clear of him but you really can't help being drawn to him.

I didn't have any expectations about what would happen next. I certainly had no intention of taking things any further – besides, I knew he was still living with Mary – so it was a simple kiss goodbye as I dropped him back at The Phene Arms.

'I'd really like to see you again, Alex,' he said.

'I'd like that too,' I replied.

Back home, Mum was cleaning the kitchen windows.

'Have you had a nice day?' she asked me as I walked in.

'Great, thanks. I've just had lunch with George Best.'

To say she was shocked would be an understatement; she nearly fell into the kitchen sink. Mum knew all about George's reputation and very colourful past because she was exactly the same age as him and had spent her twenties in Manchester when he had been a Manchester United player. I found out later that he had even been out with her sister-in-law – apparently he had picked her up in LA, where she was an air hostess and model (sound familiar?). Seeing her reaction made me play down just how attractive I had found him. I really didn't want to upset her and Dad.

I couldn't deny the attraction between us, though. George phoned me and asked to see me again and I didn't hesitate, I really wanted to see him too. He took me for lunch at the Champagne Bar at Harrods. That's more like it, I thought – sipping champagne and eating oysters. I found being in the company of this attractive older man incredibly exciting. And I loved the way he treated me, as if I was the only person in the whole world, that only I was special. He was so interested in learning everything about me – he wanted to know all about my family, my friends, my work, what I liked, what I didn't like ... I'd always felt quite nervous around John, even though we were together five years, and often felt I couldn't really open up about my feelings, but I didn't feel like that around George. He was so down to earth and easy to get along with.

After just a few more meetings we clicked. I even thought that I might have found my soul mate. I felt we really understood each other – I was communicating in a way I never had with a man before. We talked about everything – his playing days, his first marriage, his son Calum. He was a fascinating person to be with. Even though we hadn't met many times we had an intimacy between us that did feel very special to me.

Equally compelling was the physical attraction we felt for each other. 'Can't we go to a hotel? I really want make love to you,' George would repeatedly ask, and I was tempted. But I resisted. As far as I was concerned he was still living with Mary, and as long as that was the case our relationship couldn't develop. Passionate kisses would have to do for now.

I was just happy to see what unfolded with George – in no real hurry to rush into anything, enjoying our summer romance. But I hadn't bargained for George's love of publicity. On one of our dates at his local, George arranged for a photographer from a tabloid to take a picture of us together. I must have been so naïve and foolish, because I agreed without giving it a second thought. As I smiled away at the camera I had no idea of what was about to be unleashed – a tabloid feeding frenzy, the first of many in our relationship. Earlier, George had warned me about what the press could be like.

'Oh I'm used to it after five years with John Scales.' I said breezily, remembering the Britt Ekland incident.

'Alex,' George replied, 'I don't mean to be rude, but I don't think it's quite the same.'

That turned out to be the understatement of the year. The next day the story of George and the new 'leggy blonde' in his life was everywhere. When I saw my picture plastered across the tabloids, I was horrified. I really didn't want this attention. I hated seeing myself portrayed as some blonde bimbo, only interested in George because of his fame. But there was no escaping it. I tried to leave my parents' house and found it surrounded with photographers and journalists, all desperate to get a piece of me.

'Alex, tell us about you and George,' they shouted out as I ran to my car. Cameras flashed in my face. I felt hunted and I hated it. Pretty soon journalists were trawling through my life, trying to find out something juicy about the girl from Surrey. They even phoned up John, by now a very successful Liverpool player, to get him to comment about my relationship with George.

It got much worse, though. 'Hi, I've just earned fifteen grand for the story of our first night together!' It was George on the phone, sounding incredibly pleased with himself.

'What?' I shouted, in absolute disbelief. 'How could you? I don't want my parents and my grandmother reading something like that about me. You'd better phone them back right now and cancel the story.'

George sounded suitably shamed and promised to get the paper to pull the story. I couldn't believe he would behave like this. It wasn't even true – we'd restricted ourselves to kissing, and definitely hadn't had some torrid night of passion! And, even if it were true, why would he imagine I would want our private life splashed all over the papers?

George got his solicitor involved to try and stop the story, but it was no good – he didn't really have a leg to stand on, as he was the one behind the story in the first place. That weekend I was confronted by a double-page spread about our first night together, detailing in lurid detail the amazing sex we'd had. The headline was something like 'Georgy Porgy Kissed The Girls And Made Them Cry'. The article talked about how George had subsequently done a U-turn and now denied that the night of passion ever took place. It was horribly tacky. And even though I knew it wasn't true, I knew that everyone reading it would believe it.

There was no escaping the attention, though. Even when I was ten thousand feet up doing my job, I'd be aware of some of the passengers looking at me and making comments to each other as they recognised me. I could tell from their expressions they thought I was nothing more than a blonde bimbo. It was really starting to get to me.

George kept threatening to come on one of my

flights unless I agreed to see him, which filled me with dread. I was finding the press interest overwhelming, and was also deeply unsettled by not knowing what George was going to do or say next. I begged him not to, but said I was simply too stressed to meet him in Chelsea. He insisted that he would come down and meet me in a restaurant of my choice. It was quite an achievement to get George to leave the capital. However, just as I was getting ready to go out and meet him, my dad received a phone call from Mary, George's supposedly 'ex-'girlfriend. She had found out that George was meeting me for dinner and was determined to have her say about him. She was on the phone for ages, telling Dad that George was a drunk, that he'd treat me badly the way he had treated her, that I didn't know the kind of man he was, that I was too young to handle him. Needless to say, my parents were shocked. I tried to reassure them by saying there was nothing really between us. I felt so shaken by what she'd said that I was in two minds whether to go and meet George after all. But, felt I couldn't possibly stand him up if he had made the effort to come and see me. In the end I turned up half an hour late.

'I thought you'd stood me up!' George said as I sat down at the restaurant table. I couldn't even manage a smile, as I told him his girlfriend had been on the phone. George was only too eager to brush it all off. 'Don't worry about her. I've told you it's over between us.' But I knew I couldn't take things further with him as long as Mary was in his life. I also knew I couldn't bear my parents being involved like this; it was too upsetting for them.

Fortunately, I had a short break booked to Ibiza with a friend of mine. I was hoping the press interest would have died out by the time I returned home. But no, in my absence George had stoked the fires even more. As soon I walked through the front door, Mum told me I had to call John urgently. He had been commentating for Sky and had seen George, who was there recording an interview about how he had fallen madly in love with me! I felt like I was in some kind of nightmare. John knew how I would feel about that publicity and was understandably concerned. He gave me the producer's phone number, but there was no way I was up to calling them, so my mum took control.

She found out that George had just recorded the interview with Richard Keys about the love triangle in his life – Mary and me. She pleaded with the producer to stop the programme, pointing out that I barely knew George, but the answer was no. They told my mum that he had fallen for me 'hook, line and sinker', that he really loved me. As I'd only met George about four or five times I found the whole scenario totally overwhelming. Yes, he had said he loved me, but much as it had thrilled me that he had said it I hadn't really taken it seriously. I thought it was just part of the flirtation – besides, he'd only said it when he was drunk!

I sat and watched the programme with my parents, feeling shell-shocked. George did indeed confess his love for me. He also said that he loved Mary, but that he wasn't in love with her any more. He said he would accept it if she left him, and if I didn't want to know then, hard as it would be, he would accept that as well. He claimed that even if both of us left him he would cope.

He was about to find out if he could, because his interview caused two things to happen: Mary did indeed leave him and I stopped returning his calls. He was incredibly persistent and rang every day. But I backed off. Even though I had real feelings for him, I couldn't see how we could have any chance of a relationship with the amount of publicity surrounding us. Then Mary sold a story to the press. The article painted George in a very bad light. It detailed his drinking, womanising and his constant infidelities when he was with her. He had even slept with her half-sister. Mary said she had forgiven him so many times, but not any more. I was shaking by the time I finished reading it. It was too much. I couldn't become involved with this man.

CHAPTER FIVE

A BIT OF A DOWNER

'Have you got any on you?' I asked my friend hopefully. She nodded and we both made our way to the Ladies. After checking there was no one else in there, we shut ourselves in one of the cubicles, pulled down the toilet seat, gave it a quick clean and then proceeded to take a line of coke each.

I got up, rubbing my nose to make the irritation go away; my eyes streamed, but I knew that would pass. Then I took a deep breath, waiting for the delicious sensation to take hold. This drug worked only too well. It made all the bad things go away.

As we made our way back to the bar, the night suddenly felt a million times better. I was more beautiful, more articulate, more confident and so was everyone around me. The lights were sharper, brighter, the music sounded better. Best of all, I wasn't going to start brooding about George or John or any man. All better now.

I had started using coke just after I met George in July. Initially I had taken it as a way of getting over the jet lag, which I was finding increasingly difficult to cope with. Whereas a few drinks would make me sleepy, a line of coke would perk me up and I could party through the night.

Then, when the press found out about my liaison with George, I used it as a way of dealing with the stress. I'd always feel so much more relaxed when I'd taken a line or two but, in the morning, it was a different story: I would be a paranoid, shaky mess. When I stopped seeing George in August, I took it to help me forget about him. But I think as well as dealing with my conflicting feelings over George I was still getting over John. Five years is a long time and it had left its mark. He had a new girlfriend and a new life. He'd moved to Cheshire in July to be close to his new team in Liverpool and that really did make the end of our relationship seem final.

I threw myself into my single life – whenever I wasn't flying I would be socialising, going to clubs and parties in London or LA, making up for lost time after being in such a long-term relationship. On the outside I must have looked happy and carefree, but inside I was slightly going off the rails. I started to take coke more often. Instead of once a week it would be three times a week; instead of once in a night it would be twice or three times. Initially an acquaintance gave me free supplies, but, as I was developing something of an addiction, I was having to buy it myself. And it was an expensive habit.

I thought about George a lot. I hadn't spoken to him after his Sky interview. I'm not one for big confrontations, so I'd let my failure to return his calls speak for itself. He finally gave up calling me in September 1994. I told myself that I was fine, but I was in denial. I had been deeply affected by everything that had happened. I didn't share my feelings with anyone. I think all my close friends were secretly relieved that I wasn't seeing him any more, though.

Other people at Virgin were more outspoken. 'I don't know what you were doing with him anyway, he's just an old drunk, an old has-been.' People only seemed to pick up on the negative things about George. I'd just try and shrug off their criticisms, but I'd think to myself, You don't know him, you don't know what a charming, charismatic, lovely person he can be.

Until the press got their talons into the story of me and George, I hadn't realised quite what a legendary womaniser he was ... but my God he had got through them, including high-profile affairs with several Miss Worlds! Even my friend Trudie revealed that she'd had a one-night stand with George, some ten years previously. Apparently she'd gone round to his house the following day and there were three women there! Needless to say, she'd beaten a hasty retreat. But that was a side to him I hadn't seen and, apart from the press debacle, he'd been wonderful.

I still had his solid gold bracelet he'd given me and I would take it out from time to time and look at it, hoping that he was OK, wondering if I would ever see him again. On one flight I thought I saw him and my heart gave a great leap. I approached, but as I got closer I realised that it was just someone who looked like him.

I didn't want to see anyone else. Whenever I was out clubbing with my girlfriends I'd have plenty of male attention, but I wasn't interested. I didn't see anyone who compared with George. So I preferred to be single. I just wanted to enjoy my job and enjoy my time off. The trouble was, I was enjoying my time off a bit too much. Now I didn't feel I could have a good time unless I took coke. I was becoming addicted to the high it gave me. Thank God I have such good friends, because one day in December they sat me down and said, 'Alex, we're really worried about you. We think you've got a bit of a problem. You're becoming reliant on coke.'

I was shocked to hear them come out with it so bluntly. But I knew they were right. I stopped taking it there and then. I know that I have a very addictive streak in me and it would be too easy to give in to it. Even now I won't take painkillers or sleeping pills or anti-depressants because I worry I won't be able to stop. And the world didn't end when I stopped. I could still have a good time – and didn't finish up with a streaming, swollen nose every time I went clubbing!

The year 1994 ended on a much calmer note. I still thought of George and, as time had passed, the shock I'd felt about the media frenzy and George's part in it had faded. Now I only remembered the good things about the ex-footballer: how he had made me laugh; how his blue eyes had sparkled; how much I had loved spending time with him; how he had made me feel so special.

CHAPTER SIX

SECOND TIME LUCKY

January 29 1995, my 23rd birthday. I was having a joint party with Trudie, one of my closest friends, at the Dover Street Wine Bar in London. It was, and still is, one of my favourite bars, with a lovely atmosphere, friendly people and great live jazz. I was having a fabulous time, the wine was flowing freely, I was with a brilliant crowd of friends and the night was about to get a whole lot better.

'Alex, this champagne is for you.' I looked up to see the waiter placing a bottle on our table. 'It's with the gentleman's compliments.'

'What gentleman?' I asked.

Then Trudie grabbed my arm. 'Look, Alex, George is over there!'

Immediately I looked up. The man who had filled my thoughts for the last six months was indeed sitting at the bar. Our eyes met and we smiled at each other. I was so excited to see him, I had butterflies dancing in my stomach, and I could feel my heart beating wildly. I got up and walked towards him.

'Hi, thanks for the champagne.'

He wished me happy birthday and then we started talking as if the past six months hadn't happened. I can honestly say that it was wonderful to see him again.

Much as I would have liked to have carried on our conversation I couldn't abandon my friends, so after a while I said I'd have to return to my party. As he kissed me goodbye, George asked if he could phone me the next day. I had no hesitation in saying yes.

He rang in the morning and we arranged to see each other again. I felt I was totally over John, and George said that he and Mary had split up a while ago. It seemed like we'd been given a second chance. We met up for lunch at Langan's – a lovely brasserie in London, and a vast improvement on the baked-potato café we'd been to on our first date! Even after a six-month separation there was still such a good rapport between us. From that day we saw each other as often as we could, whenever my flying schedule allowed. I was falling in love with him and this time round it felt right.

We quickly became lovers and the sex was fantastic. From the very first time, George proved himself to be incredibly good in bed. I suppose that shouldn't have surprised me, given the amount of practice he'd had! He certainly knew how to please a lady and the sexual chemistry between us was very powerful. I felt intense, overwhelming desire for him. Even though he was 49, he still had a very good body, firm, athletic and muscular. The fact that we had slept together was a turning point for me; this relationship was serious.

The one downside was the fact that I couldn't tell my mum and dad about our blossoming romance. They'd been so anxious about me when all the press attention blew up after I first met George and I knew they would be worried about me getting hurt again. But I hated lying. I had always been so open about my feelings in the past and it didn't feel right sneaking off to see George without telling them where I was going and who I was seeing. I imagined telling them when the time was right, I just didn't know when that would be. As it was, someone else decided to spill the beans for me.

I had known Marco, an Italian businessman, for a couple of years, mainly through seeing him in various bars in Wimbledon. I knew he had feelings for me, which I didn't return, but I liked his company and thought he was a sweet guy. He was also incredibly generous and had bought me several Chanel suits for my birthday. In January 1995 he asked my sister and me to go on holiday to Barbados with him. He said that he would pay for everything. We said no, but he begged us, saying that he had no one else to go with. It seemed too good an offer to refuse – a chance to escape a cold, wet January in England for glorious sunshine and white-sand beaches. We went with him, but, though the location was perfect, the trip turned out to be a bit of a nightmare. He hated us going out on our own in case we got chatted up by other men and I ended up sleeping with the wardrobe against my door, because I feared he might try to come in. It only goes to show, there is no such thing as a free lunch...

Unfortunately, Marco became rather too interested in me. When he discovered that I was seeing George he became very concerned. One Sunday afternoon, I had gone to have lunch with George at Langan's, having told Mum I was somewhere else entirely. I think Marco must have been spying on me because he went marching round to Mum and Dad's.

'Do you know where Alex is?' he demanded. They replied that I was with a friend. 'No she's not, she's sitting in Langan's with George Best!' he replied angrily. To hammer home the point he called me on my mobile, telling me that he was with my parents and that they now knew exactly who I was with. Seeing the shocked look on my face, George took my mobile from me and told Marco to stop bothering me, in no uncertain terms. I was dreading facing Mum and Dad when I got home, but I shouldn't have worried; we all pretended that nothing had happened! None of us wanted to have a confrontation over this, so we simply carried on as usual.

But the great pretence couldn't continue. I was seeing George all the time and I've always been so close to my mum and told her everything, so it didn't seem right not telling her about George. He was rapidly becoming such a major part of my life. George had already introduced me to lots of his friends, including his agent Phil Hughes, who he is very close to. I think Phil was very relieved to discover that I wasn't the brainless blonde bimbo the tabloids had made me out to be.

The Saturday night before Easter Sunday, George and I had dinner at Tramp and stayed out late, so I spent the night with him at his flat in Chelsea. The next day Mum and Dad were having a family get-together and I had to be there too. To make sure I'd arrive on time I took a black cab. As we were driving through Cheam we passed Mum and Dad on their way to take the dogs out. I think they might have raised their eyebrows as if to say, 'And where have you been?' I imagine they'd worked it out, though, as you didn't usually see black cabs in Surrey.

We were all sitting down round the dinner table and were halfway through Mum's delicious Sunday roast when there was a knock at the door. I opened it and was met with the unusual sight of a chauffeur and a black limo. He handed me a bin bag, saying it was from George. Highly curious, I took it into the dining room and opened it in front of the family. Inside I discovered a beautiful Lalique glass vase, a cute teddy bear, an Easter egg, a bottle of bubbly and a letter from George, saying, 'This is what a pauper from Belfast does, I send things in black bin bags!'

I think my parents thought it a very romantic gesture in spite of the bin bag. 'I wondered where you'd been last night,' Mum said, 'now I know!' My parents could see how in love I was and so from then on they accepted the fact that I was going out with George Best. We quickly arranged to meet for dinner and though I was very nervous on the night I soon relaxed and they all got on brilliantly; Mum and Dad fell for George's charm straight away.

I couldn't have been happier; I wouldn't let anything upset me. Yes, I could see that George drank a lot, but back then I didn't think he was an alcoholic. Besides, I mainly saw him in the evenings, when everyone else was drinking too; if we met during the day for lunch he'd drink wine, but then so would I. If he got drunk he was still charming, still sexy, still someone I wanted to be with. I didn't see any dramatic mood swings in those blissful early weeks.

I didn't want to think about his past, about the different women he'd been with. The here and now was all I thought that mattered. That wasn't necessarily the view of the other women who had been part of his life. One night we were having a quiet drink in the Dover Street Wine Bar and suddenly a champagne glass came flying through the air and hit George in the face. It gave him quite a nasty cut. We were both shocked.

'What the hell was that?' I cried. The explanation soon followed in a stream of abuse from a woman standing behind us. Apparently she was his ex-girlfriend, someone he had briefly seen after the split with Mary – it seemed that George didn't like being single. She screamed and shouted at George and me, saying that he would treat me badly, just as he'd treated her. We chose not to inflame the situation and quickly left. I felt shaken but believed George when he said that she was just bitter over the break-up.

All in all, I couldn't believe how well we were getting on. I really did feel as if I'd finally met my soul mate and George told me he felt the same. I loved being with a man who was so open and passionate. He made it clear he wanted to be with me all the time, there was none of this 'I want my space'; no worry that he couldn't commit.

But it certainly wasn't all chocolate-box perfection. Quite early on in our romance, George revealed a jealous, possessive streak that took me completely by surprise. He started to hate me flying and being apart from him. In particular, he didn't like me going out when I was away. I would always phone him when I got back from a night out, not to pander to his jealousy, but because I really wanted to talk to him; I'd missed him. Usually we'd chat for hours and feel close to each other in spite of the distance. But one time when I was down route in LA and I called him I got a very different George on the line. I told him that I'd just been to the Viper Room, and what a cool club it was. He seemed very subdued, so we just chatted for a few minutes, then said goodnight. Five minutes later he phoned back in a filthy rage. He was furious that I had been to the Viper Room, saying that it was a den of iniquity, full of drugs, that River Phoenix had taken his overdose there, and asking what I was doing in a place like that. George is violently anti-drugs, so I had never told him that I'd taken cocaine, and listening to him ranting at me made me relieved I never had. Then he wanted to know who I was with and what I'd been doing. He didn't seem to accept that I'd simply been out with my girlfriends. I couldn't understand why he was making these wild accusations.

On another occasion when I was in LA he had been trying to call me in my hotel room and couldn't get through – I was on the phone to a girlfriend – and again he became enraged. When I finally spoke to him he insisted that I'd been on the phone to John. He kept going on and on about it, not letting it drop. In complete frustration I had to get my girlfriend to call him back to confirm that I had been speaking to her.

In May I went on holiday to Marbella in Spain, with my good friend Julie. Travel and sun are the perks of being an air stewardess and I was looking forward to topping up my tan and generally chilling out. At first, George was absolutely fine about me going away, then he found out that the Liverpool football team was going to be there as well, and he freaked out. He bombarded me with phone calls, convinced that I was going to be seeing John. He even insisted that John and I had secretly planned this trip to be together. That's ironic, I thought, I never went on holiday when I was with him, I'm hardly likely to be going on holiday with him now! I tried to reassure George, saying that I might bump into John, but I certainly hadn't planned the trip just to see him. There was no reasoning with him, though.

I didn't fully take it on board at the time, but I was starting to see what George could be like when he was drunk. He wasn't always the charming, loveable, funny man I knew – drink could radically change his personality and turn him into a paranoid drunk. I tried to ignore these danger signs, convinced that he would get over his jealousy. I think now I would run a mile if a man was so possessive over me, but back then I was young and naïve and so deeply in love that I was prepared to overlook everything else. Besides, George's outbursts were never for long and he was quickly back to being the man I loved.

Looking back, I realise that George was paranoid about me going off with another man because of the age gap between us. He really needn't have worried; I found him all the more attractive because he was older, because he had experienced so much and especially because he wasn't afraid to show his feelings. He had already mentioned marriage. This was no commitment phobe, this was a passionate man; one I had no intention of letting go.

I did indeed see John in Marbella, but never for an instant did I imagine being unfaithful with him. He was still as charming and good looking as he ever was, but that spark of attraction had gone out – well, on my part at least. I'm not being vain when I say that John probably would have wanted a fling for old time's sake. I'd already heard from some of his Liverpool teammates that they believed there was still a chemistry between us.

We met up one night and we did get on very well, but I'd say merely as friends who can flirt. It was a funny evening. Robbie Williams was with John and the Liverpool team. Julie had absolutely no idea who

Robbie was and was getting quite wound up by his flirtatious, cheeky behaviour. As we left she turned round and said, 'Who on earth does he think he is?' When we told her, she kicked herself.

John and one of his teammates ended up coming back to our apartment for more drinks. I told them they could stay but made it clear to John he'd be sleeping on the sofa. He looked a little put out. 'We're finished now,' I said. 'I don't want to go there any more.' And I really meant it.

I had enjoyed seeing John again, but he did have a bit of a go at me about George. 'What on earth are you doing with him?' he demanded. 'He's such a womaniser, he's got women here there and everywhere.' I was getting used to people's negative reactions. So I simply shrugged and told him it had nothing to do with him. 'Anyway, you can talk,' I added sharply. That shut John up; people in glass houses shouldn't throw stones, and all that...

There were no hard feelings, though, and in the morning we all had a pleasant breakfast together. George phoned me as he always did and after I'd finished the call John made some comment about him being keen – implying, I think, that George was trying to keep tabs on me. I felt like saying that a little more keenness on his part might have made a difference in our relationship, but I kept quiet. I already thought it ironic that John had said that it would have been nice if we could have gone on holiday when we were together! He was the one who had always made excuses about not coming away with me. It was a little late in the day to be pointing out what we could have done.

We parted on good terms, and after he'd gone I discovered that he'd left Julie and me some cash. It was very sweet of him. We'd been on such a tight budget that we'd only been able to buy the basics and we were both heartily sick of living off scrambled and boiled eggs! We immediately went out for a slap-up meal.

I enjoyed my mini-break in Spain, but I missed George intensely. It felt strange not being with him and I was longing to see him again. I didn't have long to wait. I'd just opened my front door when the phone rang. It was George.

'Are you going to come over and see me, then?' he demanded.

'Yes, of course I am but I've only just got back, I need to have a shower first!'

'Well, hurry up,' he replied.

As soon as I walked into The Phene Arms, George stood up and embraced me. It was good to see him again. Then he said, 'I've got something for you.' And he handed me a beautiful diamond engagement ring. 'Alex, will you marry me?'

My eyes filled with tears and I felt almost overwhelmed with emotion. 'Yes, I would love to marry you.' I threw my arms around his neck and kissed him passionately. The smelly old Phene Arms suddenly took on a magical glow, as I beamed at everyone. Hearing the man I loved propose to me was one of the most wonderful moments of my life.

There was a very important witness to George's proposal – Calum, George's 14-year-old son from his first marriage, who was over from the States for a visit. He seemed delighted that his dad was going to get hitched again. I don't think in any way he saw me as an evil stepmum, and we got on very well together. Inside the pub the champagne flowed, and then the three of us took off to Pucci's, an Italian restaurant on the King's Road, to celebrate our good news over pizza. I was so happy. I didn't stop smiling all night.

CHAPTER SEVEN

FOUR RUNWAYS AND A WEDDING

I was head over heels in love with George. He was 'the one', my soul mate, and my other half. I just knew we were meant to be together. I felt closer to him than I had felt to any other man, and that summer I made love with a man as I never had before – sex was intense and passionate. We really were that annoying couple that can't keep their eyes or hands off each other! Frequently when we were out we would get carried away and have to sneak off for a quickie. I'm ashamed to say we even managed it in the Ladies of the Phene – which only goes to show how loved up I was, because it was not a location I would normally choose! Then, one hot summer night, we slipped out into the beer garden and made love there. George's flat was only a few minutes away, but we just couldn't wait a second longer.

I couldn't wait to be married to this man. I think we

both believed that, once we were married, people would be more accepting of our relationship and stop obsessing over the older man with his young blonde girlfriend and start to see us for what we were – a couple who were deeply in love. Mum and Dad were the first to congratulate us; they never made any comments about the age difference.

Even during those heady, happy weeks following George's proposal, however, he tested the strength of my love for him. In June I had a hectic flying schedule and was feeling increasingly exhausted with jet lag. When I returned from one particular trip I was so tired I went straight home and crawled into bed. I was supposed to be meeting George that night, but I slept right through my alarm. At 2am I was woken by a phone call.

'Where the hell have you been?' It was George. He was drunk and raving. I tried to explain what had happened but he was having none of it. 'Anyway, I've met someone really special and she's with me now. Go on, Louisa, say hello to Alex.' And to my absolute horror he tried to get a woman he was with to come to the phone.

I could hardly believe what I was hearing and, as there was no reasoning with him, I just said, 'If that's what you want to do, then goodbye.' I slammed the phone down and collapsed on the bed, the tears streaming down my face. My dreams of marrying this man were shattered.

We didn't speak for a week. I was torn between

missing him and being furious. George bombarded me with calls, but I really didn't want to speak to him. But the more I ignored him, the more he begged me to come back. Finally I picked up the phone and called him. He told me he was sorry, that nothing had happened between him and the girl, and that he'd just used her to wind me up because I hadn't met him and he didn't know what I was doing.

I took a deep breath. 'I'll come back if you promise to stop behaving like this and if you promise to calm down your drinking.' It was the first time I had spoken about his drinking. I didn't realise it at the time, but it would become my mantra for the next nine years.

'I swear I will, Alex. Please come back. I love you.'

We had a passionate reconciliation and George was true to his word, and really did seem to cut down on the booze. We even booked in to Henlow Grange health farm for a week because he said he wanted to get into shape for our big day. Everything seemed to be back on track. I could continue being the excited bride-to-be, though we hadn't set a date yet. I imagined we'd be married in a couple of months' time. George had different ideas, though.

I was having my hair done when my mobile rang.

'Right kid, we're getting married next week.'

I let out a whoop of delight, startling my hairdresser.

'I've just spent the last four hours standing in a queue at the Chelsea Register Office. We're booked in for next Monday morning at ten.'

I was totally bowled over. I had never wanted a

traditional church wedding anyway, and tying the knot so spontaneously seemed wonderfully romantic. Besides, the Chelsea Register was a great old building with plenty of character, where lots of stars had got married in the past.

The week passed in a frenzy of planning. George's friends organised the reception and the cake; The Phene Arms promised to lay on canapés and champagne immediately after the ceremony – well, as George had probably single-handedly been boosting their profits over the years, it was the least they could do! And I scoured the shops for the perfect dress.

I finally found it in Whistles. It was a beautifully elegant slip dress by the designer Ghost. Its pale-caramel colour perfectly complemented my golden tan and blonde hair. I had never wanted to get married in white and definitely didn't long to parade around in some meringue-style wedding dress with a veil.

As it was shaping up to be such a gloriously hot summer, I decided I wanted to go for a *Midsummer Night's Dream* theme and so ordered a lovely wreath for my hair, with cream roses and red berries, a matching posy and matching buttonholes for the men.

Then there was just the matter of George's ring. I didn't exactly have a great deal of money, so opted for a simple signet ring with our initials engraved on it. George got me a beautiful gold band, twisted in the middle with six diamonds from Mappin & Webb.

Every day that week I woke up with a feeling of delicious anticipation. Because we were getting married so quickly there was no time for the agonising over guest lists and menus that can go along with a couple's big day; we could just concentrate on what mattered – us. Two days before we got married, George lined up a special treat. He whisked me up to Manchester to see a concert given by an old friend of his.

'How did you manage to trap him, then?' Rod Stewart asked me, as George introduced us in the bar of the Midland Hotel. For a moment I was a little starstruck and then I relaxed. Rod was very down to earth and easy to talk to. George knew him from way back in the Sixties. I was starting to realise that George knew everybody!

'Hurry up,' someone called out to Rod. 'You're on soon.'

'Well,' he retorted, 'they can't start without me, can they?'

It was a brilliant night. Rod gave a great performance and as he belted out his numbers I kept looking at George and thinking, Only two more days to go! After the gig we shared a few more drinks with Rod; I was relieved to see that George's drinking was under control. As we left the bar to go to bed Rod serenaded us with 'Who's Getting Married in the Morning'. It was a great night.

The following evening we met my family for dinner at Scalinis, one of our favourite restaurants on the Walton Road. George's family couldn't come over from Ireland for the wedding because it was simply too short notice, but my family made up for it and they all seemed delighted for us.

I was determined that nothing should go wrong for our big day, so that night after George had fallen asleep I snuck out of bed, locked the front door of the flat and hid the keys. Now he couldn't escape! It might sound like a strange thing to do the night before your wedding, but several times that summer I had woken in the night and discovered that George wasn't in bed with me, or even in the flat. He'd come back around 5am a little the worse for wear, saying he had gone to Tramp because he couldn't sleep. Well, I definitely didn't want him doing that tonight! I crept back into bed and curled round him.

The next morning it was the most glorious summer day. It turned out to be the hottest day of the year, in fact. I leaped out of bed and started getting ready. When George saw me in my wedding dress, he kissed me and said I looked beautiful. He was, however, rather put out to discover that the shoes I was wearing meant that I was a couple of inches taller than him! But I told him he'd have to live with it – the shoes matched my dress perfectly and they were staying.

Just before ten the car arrived to take us to the ceremony. It was a metallic blue open-topped Bugatti and extremely stylish. We had no opportunity to sit back and enjoy the ride, as Chelsea Register Office was literally round the corner from George's flat! But no girl wants to walk to her wedding ceremony – it's essential to arrive in style.

Apart from my family and a couple of George's very close friends we only gave our guests two days' notice

With footballer and former boyfriend John Scales and the dog he gave me for my 19th birthday, Seve.

Above: With Richard Branson, the day I was awarded my 'wings' by Virgin Atlantic.

Below: Some early modelling shots.

The first shot of George
and I, taken shortly
after we met.

Although our wedding wasn't a huge, lavish affair, we all certainly had fun …

Above left: In my beautiful wedding dress, made by Ghost. My headdress and bouquet had a hint of *A Midsummer Night's Dream* about them.

Above right: A kiss from my groom.

Below left: George and I with my family.

Below right: With my best friends – and bridal attendants – Trudie (*left*) and Julie (*right*).

Post-marital activities for the newlyweds. *Above left*: A different kind of ball game for George.

Above right: George presenting awards at a charity football match –I got the best prize.

Below: Nice shell suits! Keeping dry at Niagara Falls.

Above: A night out with footballing greats. *From left to right*, Jimmy Greaves, Denis Law, George and agent Alan Platt.

Below: George and I with Johnny Gold, who owns the nightclub Tramp, where George and I first met.

Despite our problems, George and I had some wonderful times seeing the world.

Above: On holiday with my parents in Portugal.

Below left: Wrapped up for the chillier climes of Switzerland.

Below right: When the *Mail on Sunday* offered to fly us anywhere in the world for an interview, my wish came true when we were whisked away to magical Mustique.

George after being awarded *Loaded*'s Rogue of the Year award in 1999.

of our wedding. We really wanted the day to be a private celebration and didn't want hordes of press descending on us. George and I had no desire either to do an *OK!* or *Hello!* photoshoot of our big day. I think those shoots are terribly impersonal and, besides, I wanted to enjoy myself, not feel I had to pose for endless photographs.

As a precaution we went into the register office through the side entrance. Once there we discovered that Rod Stewart and his wife Rachel Hunter had sent us a beautiful bouquet of flowers. I could feel the nerves and excitement building up in me. I had been dreading saying my vows because I couldn't say 'solemnly'. George kept saying, 'Just say solemn (pause) lee!' But I thought it made me sound like a halfwit. In the end I did manage to take George Best to be my lawfully wedded husband without slipping up on the words, though my voice was quivering and my left leg was inexplicably shaking. At least I didn't have a Princess Diana moment over his middle name – he doesn't have one.

George was obviously affected by nerves as well, because he tried to put his ring on my finger. 'Hang on,' I said, 'I need my ring.' I had no intention of wearing a signet ring for the rest of my married life. I wanted the diamonds!

We left by the side entrance, but there was a freelance photographer there and he managed to get a picture of us. But I didn't mind. I was Mrs Best now. We went to the Phene as arranged for our glass of celebratory champagne, but the landlord had obviously forgotten all about it. He was dressed in his shorts, doing DIY behind the bar and there wasn't a glass of champagne or a canapé in sight. In fact, the only thing he could offer us was lukewarm white wine – hardly what we wanted to toast our nuptials. We hastily got in our cars and headed off to the reception.

George's friends had arranged the reception at a lovely old-fashioned pub on the outskirts of London. Unfortunately, it was bang on the doorstep of Heathrow Airport, practically at the end of a runway! So our celebrations were punctuated by the sounds of planes taking off and landing. Denis Law, a close friend of George's from his playing days, wittily called it 'Four Runways and a Wedding'! And it was a little disconcerting for me, as I was actually supposed to be working and I'd had to phone in sick, as it was much too short notice to take leave. I even saw the Virgin plane I was supposed to be on flying really low overhead and could just imagine the crew winching a little ladder out to pick me up and get me on board.

The noise aside, it was a fabulous day. The buffet was fantastic, the wine flowed, the weather was gorgeous and there was a great band playing sixties songs. All our guests, without exception, said that it was one of the best weddings they had ever been to because it was so fun and informal. And I loved the fact that the day had been so unconventional – it seemed to reflect my relationship with George. My dad hates public speaking, so his best friend, Ian, a family friend I had known all my life, stood in for him. George made such a moving speech. He said that he really didn't have any choice but to marry me, because he loved me so much; how as soon as he met me he wanted to marry me and for me to have his name; and how he wanted to take care of me forever. Of course, then he ruined it all by falling off the stage a little the worse for wear, which had us all in hysterics. Even a few hours into our marriage I was been given a hint of what to expect – the sublime followed by the ridiculous...

By six o clock we were partied out, the early start, blazing sun and alcohol had taken their toll. George and I stopped off at Pucci's for a quick bite to eat on our way home and then we had to go straight back to bed because we were exhausted! But at half-past one we both woke up feeling refreshed.

'Do you fancy going out, Bestie?' George asked me. Married, I had gained the nickname I gave him.

'I'd love to,' I replied, getting up and putting on my wedding dress.

Then the two of us headed off to Tramp, where we had a glass of champagne with our friend Johnny Gold. As we walked into the bar, lots of people called out, 'Congratulations!' The morning papers had just come out and we had made the front page of the *Express*. It was not the first time we made the headlines, but at least this was one of the happiest times, and one I will always cherish.

CHAPTER EIGHT

THE NEW MRS BEST

The day following our wedding set the pattern for our married life: don't expect things to be conventional. George and I were enjoying our first breakfast together as man and wife when there was a loud knock on the door. It was one of the regulars from The Phene Arms in a complete state, because the bailiffs had come round threatening to close down the pub and the landlord was nowhere to be found. Immediately, George leaped into action. I already knew what a fan he was of his local, as we'd shared so many of our intimate moments in there, so it was no surprise when he seized a wad of cash and set off to rescue his beloved pub. It wasn't exactly how I had imagined our first morning together as a married couple, but then I had expected our life to be different from that of other couples. George wasn't like other men, and this was one of the many reasons I fell in love with him. I suppose I hadn't quite bargained for how different, though…

George paid off the bailiffs and sat down to have a glass of water. By now the press had seized on the fact that he was a married man and so had a field day when they discovered he was drinking in his local the day after his wedding! They chose to ignore the fact that this was the rare occasion when he was only knocking back water. After he had successfully bailed out his pub, he returned home and we set off for a celebratory lunch with Johnny Gold and his wife at the Belvedere, an exclusive restaurant in Holland Park. I was feeling like a blissed-out bride and kept holding my hand up and admiring my wedding ring.

That week I moved my things into George's flat and went shopping with my mum to buy our wedding present from her and Dad. I've always had a bit of a weakness for clothes and before we looked at things for the marital home I had a quick look in one of my favourite designer shops in Wimbledon village. There I spotted a gorgeous cream suede skirt and matching jacket. I tried it on and knew I had to have it. I quickly phoned George. 'Would you mind if my parents' wedding present to us was a new outfit for me?' He laughed and said it was fine by him. Neither of us had made a big deal about wedding presents – we hadn't sent out a list because we only gave our guests two days' notice – but we ended up with some lovely gifts. Some of the guests were obviously psychic, because they bought cookbooks – they must have known how much of my married life I would spend in the kitchen!

We couldn't go off on honeymoon because George

had too many work commitments. So, two weeks after the wedding, instead of honeymooning with George I flew to Portugal with Phil his manager, Phil's girlfriend and Denis Law. George urged me to go, saying that he'd be busy anyway, and promising that we could go off on honeymoon at a later date.

It was a terrible mistake to leave him on his own. While I was away he started drinking heavily again. He ended up missing all his work engagements and phoned me every night in a drunken, incoherent state. He'd call all night. I was desperately worried about him, but in the end we had to take the phone out of the socket because none of us was getting any sleep. It was misery not being able to see him and make sure he was all right. Hardly the carefree break in the sun we had all planned. Looking back, I realise George wanted me to go away because he wanted to drink.

By the time we returned George was fully immersed in one of his 'benders'. It was the first time I had seen him drinking this much and it was a shock. Phil and I walked into the Phene and there he was sitting at his regular table, an enormous glass of white wine in front of him. He was very, very drunk. We managed to get him home, where he collapsed in bed. I had been looking forward to our reunion when I was in Portugal, wanting to make love with my new husband, but there was no chance of that in the state he was in. I got into bed beside him and put my arms around him, but George didn't even register my presence. 'I love you,' I said. But he didn't wake up.

The following morning, there was no explanation from him, no apology, no promise to stop drinking. He simply gave me a kiss, said he'd see me later and headed off to the Phene, oblivious to everything except his need for a drink. It was hardly my idea of married bliss. But I didn't cry, I tried to pretend it wasn't happening and prayed that it would all blow over and he'd be back to normal. Even this early on in our marriage I knew him well enough to know that having a go at him about his drinking was not going to get him to stop.

So every day for the next two weeks, George would skip breakfast and be in the pub drinking white wine at ten o'clock in the morning. He would stagger home at four in the afternoon, collapse into bed for a nap and then return to the pub. When he finally came back in the evening he was paralytic and could only pass out in a drunken stupor. I hated seeing him like this. I felt so helpless and alone. The last thing I wanted to do was tell my family and friends what was going on – it hardly showed my marriage in a good light. So I kept it all to myself.

But I did discover what was to prove a very useful survival tactic in the years that followed. Rather than waiting for him to come home to me, it was better for me to go out, to see my friends, to keep busy. George didn't like coming back to the flat and finding it empty. He started to wonder where I was and what I was doing and finally he stopped drinking.

'Come on, kid,' he said one morning, 'let's go to the health farm.' And so it was off to Henlow Grange for

George's liver to have a brief rest. It was lovely having the sober George back and we quickly resumed our passionate, loving relationship. I was only too happy to forgive and forget the previous weeks. Back then I was optimistic enough to think that they might be one-offs. I didn't for one second imagine that George's drinking would define and ultimately destroy our marriage.

Our stay at the health farm helped George stop drinking because he was away from the temptation of the local pub, but I'm definitely not a health-farm kind of girl. I would have been fine just for a weekend, but George wanted to spend a couple of weeks away and there's only so many pampering treatments you can have before you start feeling totally overindulged – and, I'm afraid to say, a little bored. I ended up befriending the local farmer and spent a lot of time down on the farm, collecting the eggs and checking on the animals. I even helped him deliver a calf. Well, it beat sipping hot water and wandering around in a white towelling dressing gown all day!

Then it was back to Chelsea for a detoxed George and a slightly stir-crazy me. It was great to be back in the city and I absolutely loved living in Chelsea with its vibrant bars and restaurants – and, of course, fantastic shops. It wasn't quite so good to be back in our tiny flat. George had been one of the greatest footballers of all time, better than Beckham, probably on a level with Pele, but he certainly hadn't got the lifestyle that you might expect. He'd earned a fortune in his time and blown it. True, he lived in Chelsea, a very wealthy area, but George only had a two-bedroomed flat. And this was all the property he had – there was no country mansion, no holiday home somewhere exotic. When I saw the flat for the first time it was a shock. This was no luxury bachelor pad, just a basement flat that had seen better days. The decor was shabby and looked as if it hadn't been touched since the Sixties; the grey carpets were threadbare and the furniture was falling apart. The boiler didn't work properly and in the summer you could only get hot water if the heating was on, so if I wanted a bath the flat would end up sweltering and there wasn't even a garden to cool down in. The kitchen was so small it could barely fit two people. There wasn't even a washing machine! For years George had employed a man named Martin as his cleaner and general gofer, and he would traipse off to the launderette for us, but I really didn't want him washing my underwear, so I would end up hand-washing it in the sink – hardly something you can imagine Mrs Beckham doing! So, if the press imagined me swanning around like a stereotypical footballer's wife, with nothing on my mind except shopping for designer clothes, getting my hair and nails done and generally living in the lap of luxury, they couldn't have been more wrong.

I think even my friends and family were surprised by just how little George owned. My mum had even suggested that we hold the wedding reception at George's house. I had smiled and replied, 'I don't think so, Mum, George has only got a flat!'

This was the marital home, however, and I knew I had better get used to it. It did feel a little strange at first, as George had lived there with Mary. I don't think anyone exactly welcomes living somewhere a previous relationship has taken place. My first purchase was a new mattress and new bed linen; the furniture and paintwork might have to wait, but I certainly wasn't going to start married life under another woman's duvet.

What I couldn't get used to was George's obsession with drink and his constant desire to be at The Phene Arms. It was becoming clearer that he was an alcoholic – not that he would admit it, and not that I really wanted to either. He kept saying that he could give up drinking at any time and I had hoped after his binge that he really would cut down; I wasn't expecting him to stop. 'Cutting down' for him still meant going to the pub every day, all day, if he wasn't working, and drinking all day – it's just that he wouldn't get quite so paralytic as he would on a binge. I now understood why he hadn't done much to the flat: he only came back to sleep – the Phene was basically his office and his living room. If anybody ever wanted to get hold of him, they would phone the pub. Inside the local he was treated as a kind of god; everything he said went and he would hold court, surrounded by admiring old men, who could all remember what a sublimely talented footballer he had been. Meanwhile, back home he had a young wife who desperately wanted to be with her husband. Much as I loved George there was no way I wanted to spend all my time in the pub.

In August I was due to do a flight and I really didn't want to go. When I turned up for work I was delighted to discover that they had double-booked my place and so I wasn't needed. As soon as I got home I made the phone call I had been intending to make for several weeks, to hand in my notice. Virgin were very sorry to lose me but my flying days were over.

George had already said that when we were married he wanted me to retire, that he didn't want me flying off here, there and everywhere without him. And I was only too happy to give up being an air stewardess. I was getting bored of it. I'd been flying for a year and a half, and although I'd had some great times it was not an ideal job when you're married. George found my absences very difficult and would inevitably become paranoid about me going off with a handsome pilot. I planned to do the odd spot of modelling if the right job came up, but I had no wish to have a full-time career as a model. It's not a very 21st-century thing to admit, and I'm sure feminists would be up in arms, but I wanted to be a traditional wife and look after my husband, as I'd seen my mum look after my dad. I also hoped that if I wasn't working I would be able to keep tabs on George's drinking and perhaps even break his dependence on The Phene Arms. I think I saw it as a challenge. Unfortunately, it was never going to be a challenge I could win.

Looking after George was going to be my nine-to-five job, plus overtime. First of all I decided to learn to cook. I had rarely spent much time in the kitchen before, but now I was determined to have a home-cooked meal on the table every night for my husband. And I was going to cook from scratch; I wasn't going to cheat and buy ready-made meals. So I began my new career as Alex Best, domestic goddess. I was genuinely happy, pottering off to Waitrose to buy fresh ingredients, then surprising George with my latest creation. I think he found it amazing that someone would actually cook for him. He would even take the shepherd's pies I had made into the pub to share with the regulars and generally boast about my cooking.

Cooking was a good distraction for me as well. I had hoped that when I gave up work George and I would spend more time together, but if we were in Chelsea he had his routine mapped out and nothing, not even me, was going to stop him following it. Most men would get up and go to work; George got up and went to the pub. From there he would go to Pucci's for a snack, then on to the bar Henry J Beans, then on to the betting shop, then back to the Phene. He'd return home at four for a nap, then go out again to the pub until seven-thirty, when he would finally return home for dinner.

There were times in those early months of married life when I felt very lonely. All my friends were at work, so I could only meet them briefly for lunch. My mum was a great support and she would often travel up and spend the day with me, or I would go down and see her. I'm a very sociable person and, while I don't mind my own company, there's only so much of it I want to have. It was no good saying anything to George as he'd just say come to the pub. I kept myself busy, though – I got a personal trainer and ran at least three miles every day. Of course, I cooked too, and to while away some of the long afternoons when George was holding court in the pub I became something of a shopaholic. I ended up with a wardrobe bulging with clothes and shoes, some of which I never even wore and ended giving up to a friend's daughter a year or so later.

I was becoming increasingly worried about George's chaotic financial affairs. He was incredibly irresponsible about money, clueless about budgeting, or paying bills, or setting aside money for his tax bills. He demanded to be paid in cash for any work that he did, and would then end up spending it and forgetting that he still had bills to pay. He seemed to love going round with a huge wad of cash – it was not unusual for him to carry several thousand pounds at a time. George was quite childlike in wanting to show off 'his readies', as he called them. I'm sure he ended up getting robbed more than once and I found it very embarrassing when he flashed his cash around. He'd already been made bankrupt several years earlier and now he seemed to be heading down another path toward financial disaster.

He was receiving frequent letters from the bailiffs and I'd already had several nasty surprises when I'd gone to open the front door and found men threatening to take our furniture away for unpaid bills. It was extremely stressful. That said, I had to smile when I recalled how the press had depicted me as some kind of gold-digging bimbo, only interested in marrying George for his fame and his money! While he was by no means destitute, he certainly wasn't rolling in it. Put it this way, if money had been my sole motivation I would have been better off steering well clear of George. As he said in one of his autobiographies, 'I was no great catch.'

Fortunately, my dad put me in touch with a very good accountant and we started trying to make sense of the mess. I opened a joint bank account and made sure that George was given cheques for his work plus VAT and that they were handed directly to me. George had never done a VAT return and owed a fortune. I think he thought the VAT was just more money for him to spend! It took me the next five years to sort out his VAT. Like I said, there would have been easier ways of marrying my fortune!

At that time his main source of income came from his stage shows and after-dinner speeches. And George did very well from these dinners, recounting stories about his legendary playing days and his very colourful love life. He would often have several bookings a week. Now I was no longer flying we decided that I would keep a diary of his work engagements, act as his PA and accompany him on his trips. Usually we'd be put up in good-quality hotels and the venues would be very pleasant, although that wasn't always the case. In those days George wasn't terribly discerning about the kind of work he'd accept and some of the bookings were in complete dives, grotty working men's clubs, where he didn't even get paid very much. First of all, of course, Phil and I had the thankless task of getting him to the gig, and that would mean dragging him out of The Phene Arms.

'Come on, George,' I'd say. 'The car's here, we've got to go!'

'OK, in a minute, I'll just have one more.'

I would stand there feeling more and more wound up, as one more became two more, then three more. And by then we were hopelessly late.

We travelled all over the country and spent hours on trains going to places such as Grimsby or Worksop. It was not glamorous. If George was sober, his speeches would be brilliant, full of entertaining anecdotes about his playing days. I was less keen on hearing yet again about the Miss Worlds he'd bedded and the numerous other beauty queens. I hated people watching me, wondering how I could bear to listen to my husband's former sexual exploits. But, if he was drunk, his speeches would be a disaster and I would literally sit there cringing. He would forget his stories, ramble on and basically make a fool of himself. Part of the problem was that George is quite a shy person and would often feel that he needed a drink beforehand to give him confidence. But sometimes he couldn't leave it at one. Often the organisers would be at fault because they would have a wine waitress behind him, constantly refilling his glass. I'd spend the whole time trying to monitor his drinking, swapping his full glass for a half-empty one when he wasn't looking. Then, if he did end up drunk, the organisers would have a go at me! I rapidly grew more thick-skinned, but even when things went wrong I would still much rather have been with George than away from him. I knew I had made the right decision in giving up my job.

A month after we were married, George landed a job on Sky as a football pundit on their Saturday sports programme. I was delighted for him. It was great money, regular work and, as it was football, something he was passionate about, I hoped it would give him a good incentive not to drink. I was convinced that part of the reason George drank was because he got bored. I guess that, after being one of the world's greatest players, everything else in life must be a bit of an anticlimax.

The first Saturday he insisted I go with him because he was so nervous. I even made him a thermos of soup and a packed lunch, as if for a school boy on his first day at school. But he needn't have worried. He was brilliant; even I could see that much, with my pitiful amount of football knowledge.

I had married George because I loved him – it had nothing to do with his fame. I never thought of myself as being married to George Best, the footballing legend – he was simply the man I loved. And we really didn't have a 'celebrity' lifestyle that revolved around going to premieres and parties. We received plenty of invitations to go to such events, but George never wanted to go and neither did I – we would much rather socialise with our close friends and family.

Of course, George did know his fair share of celebs, some of whom were close friends. One of those was Michael Parkinson and that summer I got my first taste of rubbing shoulders with the stars. Every year Michael holds a cricketing party and lines up a celebrity team to play his local cricket team. I had a modelling job in the morning of the party and so had to meet George and my parents there. When I arrived I felt a little shy as I mingled with the likes of Chris Tarrant and Gary Lineker, but that feeling soon vanished when I discovered that George was on top form; he was sober, he played some great cricket, and he was wonderful company. On days like this I knew I had made the right decision when I married him.

I had been longing to meet George's family, but it wasn't until October that George finally took me over to Belfast. It was a bit of an eye-opener for me. By then it was the time of the ceasefire and so the city was beginning to be a safer place, but there were still checkpoints at the airport and at the hotel and I did feel slightly nervous. I also really wanted to get on with George's family, as I knew how important they were to him.

George comes from a very different background from me. He is the oldest of six and comes from a working-class Protestant family and was brought up on a council estate. I believe he had a very happy childhood, though quite a short one, as by the age of 15 he had joined Manchester United's youth team and had moved away from home. Sadly, his mum had died in 1978. George told me that she had been an alcoholic; she had found George's fame very difficult to deal with. George got treated – and still gets treated – like a god in Ireland, but there were always people who would say, 'Who does he think he is?' and his mum found it particularly hurtful. There is a belief that alcoholism runs in families, that it is genetic. I just prayed that George was strong enough to break that link.

I had the warmest possible welcome from George's family. Everyone seemed so genuinely pleased to meet me and delighted that George and I were married. Dickie, George's dad, was lovely, a very quiet and gentle man but one who clearly didn't put up with any nonsense. He made it clear to me that he knew exactly what George was like and that I shouldn't put up with any nonsense either! My only problem with Dickie was that it took me a while to tune into his accent; initially I couldn't understand a word he said, as he spoke so quietly and so quickly.

It was clear that George came from a very close-knit family and every Thursday afternoon all the children would come round for tea at Dickie's house, which was when I was introduced to them all. One by one they came into the front room and said their hellos, then George's little five-year-old niece Ashleigh came racing in shouting, 'Where's Alex? I want to meet her.' As soon as she saw me she gave me an enormous hug and kiss and said, 'I love you!' I had tears in my eyes. It was lovely to be greeted like this and particularly special because Ashleigh wasn't a very well little girl at all. She had hydrocephalus, or water on the brain.

George was always telling me stories about his childhood and while we were in Ireland he was determined to show me some of the places that had been special to him. One of these had been a place called Pickie Pool, a little seaside resort in Bangor where the family would go for day trips. While his mum played bingo, he and the others would roam on the beach, eating ice creams, building sandcastles and generally have a great time. He was desperate to show the place to me, so we planned our own day trip there.

George had been upset at the enormous white limousine we'd been given to drive us around. When he goes home he likes to blend in, not come across as some big star – the trouble is, that's how most of Ireland sees him! He'd already been mortified when we went to have tea at his dad's and this ostentatious car had waited for us outside his dad's council house. On our trip to the seaside, George was so paranoid about being seen getting out of the car that he insisted we were dropped off miles away from the beach. Unfortunately, his childhood idyll had changed beyond recognition and after a long, cold walk we discovered the simple beach had become a big flashy marina, so our journey had been in vain.

Overall, though, our trip to Ireland had been a great success. I loved meeting George's family because it was like discovering a part of him that I hadn't known before – and it was a very good part. It made me think optimistically of the future: of one day starting our own family.

CHAPTER NINE

FOR BETTER, FOR WORSE

One of the great things about being with George was that I never quite knew where we were going to end up next. He would get invited all over the world to give speeches and coaching exhibitions, to open hotels or restaurants. I loved the unpredictability of it all, especially after the routine of living in Chelsea, where I knew exactly what would happen every day.

In April 1996 we went off to New Zealand for ten days, where George was to tour and give some speeches. We had one of the happiest trips of our marriage there. George stayed sober for the entire visit and I was so proud of my clever, funny husband, who worked his socks off and who entertained and charmed everyone he met. When he was like this it was easy to forget the bad times, and I willingly did.

We stayed in a luxury five-star hotel in Auckland, though there was one drawback. Every day and night we would hear the sound of piano music from the suite upstairs. Tuneful as the music was, it was starting to drive us slightly barmy. Then we discovered it was Dudley Moore and suddenly it didn't seem so annoying after all! George slipped a note under his door and the three of us met up one morning. Dudley was yet another person George had come to know over the years and he was great company.

On the return home we stopped off in Malaysia and stayed at the Hilton Hotel, as George was opening a restaurant there. I felt so close to George that part of me didn't want to go back to London. I didn't want to lose this sober, lovely man. Away from the influence of the pub we were like new lovers again. It was a precious time.

Back home, George had something to focus on – his 50th birthday, on 22 May 1996. BBC2 was going to devote an entire evening to documentaries about his life, including a live interview with him. I also had to give my first ever television interview about my life with George. I was so nervous that I kept having to do re-takes – they must have loved me in the edit suite.

Then we received tragic news from Ireland. George's niece Ashleigh had died after a seizure. We were both terribly upset by the news. She had been so full of life, and laughter and love and when she died she was only seven years old. I had worried that the news might cause him to drink, but he didn't. He managed to contain his grief and gave a good performance on television. A few days later we held a huge party for him at a club in Piccadilly called Football, Football. Lots of George's friends turned up, including Michael Parkinson, Des Lynam, Gary Rhodes and Jimmy Tarbuck, and George again made a special effort not to drink. He could obviously see how much trouble everyone had gone to for him and he didn't want to spoil things. I also think that he and quite a few other people were amazed that he'd got to fifty at all.

As George was celebrating this milestone in his life, however, I was beginning to find that married life was something of a roller coaster. Increasingly, George's drinking was leading us to have rows. Drunk, he was starting to become unreasonable and aggressive. He seemed to delight in picking fights with me and his favourite subject would be that I had been flirting with other men. He would become very jealous and possessive, hating me even talking to another man, however innocently. And it always was innocently – I wasn't interested in anyone but George. I couldn't understand why he was driving a wedge between us. His behaviour became so unreasonable that I even had to stop going out with my girlfriends. The consequences of me having a few drinks and a catch-up were too much to put up with. If ever I did go out, I'd be met with World War Three on my return and a hostile barrage of 'Where have you been?' and 'Who have you been seeing?' Alternatively, he wouldn't talk to me for two weeks.

It began to seem that I could only see my friends if George and I had argued and then I'd storm out and pick up my social life – hardly a healthy situation. I'd meet up with my friends at Café de Paris or go to Stringfellows, and while it was great to see them, it was horrible knowing that I was only out because I'd had an argument with my husband; it took the shine off the night.

These rows paled into insignificance in June 1996. We hadn't even been married a year when George did something that made me question whether we had any kind of future together.

'Oh my God, what was that?' I sat up suddenly in bed. I had felt something moving on my face. I looked round frantically, but George wasn't there. Then my attention was caught by something on the floor. I looked more closely and saw several large clumps of blonde hair. Instantly, I put my hand on my head. My fringe had been hacked off and I could feel that large chunks of the rest of my hair had been cut.

Then I saw a large kitchen knife and a pair of scissors on the bedside table. 'Jesus Christ!' I leaped out of bed and looked at my face in the mirror. I gasped in horror at the reflection staring back at me. My beautiful hair had been mutilated and my face and body were covered with incomprehensible scribbles made with a black marker pen. I felt a huge surge of anger and raced into the living room. George was lying on the sofa, drunk.

'What the hell have you done to me?' I screamed at him. 'Look at the state of my hair! Why did you do it?'

George mumbled incoherently, and it was clear that he didn't know what to say.

'Come on,' I yelled. 'What made you do this to me? You've got to tell me!'

But George couldn't or wouldn't answer. I was beside myself, furious but also shaken. It made me wonder just what he was capable of and whether he actually had any control over his actions. One thing was certain: I couldn't bear to stay in the flat a moment longer. I picked up the phone and dialled a number. Please answer it, I prayed. Please.

'Dad, can you come and pick me up?' My voice trembled with emotion and the strain of trying not to cry.

George wouldn't even look at me. I went into the bathroom and started trying to scrub the marker pen off my face and body. A few minutes later I heard the front door close. George had left, obviously too ashamed to face my dad or me.

As soon as Dad arrived, I gave in to the tears. He was shocked by the state of me, and I hated him seeing me like this. I had no wish to involve my parents in my marriage difficulties, but I had to get away.

For four days I stayed with my parents. I was terribly upset, questioning whether I could even stay with the man who could do this to me. And I couldn't help thinking about an even more frightening scenario: what if he stabbed me in a drunken rage? I felt incredibly stressed: I couldn't eat, couldn't sleep, the thoughts tumbled round in my head. I loved George and I knew he loved me, so what was going on?

In the middle of the emotional turmoil I had the highly embarrassing situation of going to the hairdressers to try and get my hair sorted out. When they asked me what on earth I'd done to it, I lied and said a friend's child got a bit carried away – well, I could hardly admit it was my husband, could I? I ended up with a hideous mullet cut and every time I looked at myself in the mirror I felt angry and upset. Hair is, after all, a woman's crowning glory and I really didn't think I could forgive George for sabotaging mine. I'd always thought we could survive anything because we were so deeply in love and I believed that would be enough. Unfortunately, this time round I wasn't sure that it was.

George called all the time, apologising for what he had done, promising to make it up to me. He gave no explanation for his actions; I don't think he could even remember doing it. Lately he had been drinking heavily again, on one of his bad benders. I could only guess that his jealous paranoia had got the better of him.

'Please, Alex, can I see you?' It was the fifth time he'd rung that day, the fourth day we had been apart. I hesitated. 'Please, I really miss you,' he said again.

'OK,' I replied, 'But not at the flat.'

'I'll come down, take you out for dinner.'

As I got ready, I felt broken-hearted. That morning, after another sleepless night, I had made the momentous decision to leave George. But as soon as I saw him again, waiting for me in the restaurant, as soon as he put his arms round me and kissed me, I knew that I couldn't. I loved him and, for better, for worse, he was the man I wanted to spend the rest of my life with.

I looked at him across the table and took a deep

breath. 'I'll come back, but you've got to promise not to behave like this again.'

'I will, I swear I will,' came his fervent answer. And I believed him. I wanted to.

I moved back to the flat, but things were still a little raw between us; George had shaken my trust in him. The very first thing I did was to hide all the kitchen knives – the thought of him getting out of control with a knife when drunk was too alarming to imagine. Initially George was full of apologies, and obviously wanted us to forget what he'd done, but he didn't exactly go on to become a model husband.

As if I didn't have enough to worry about with his drinking, he started to become very flirtatious with a couple of barmaids at The Phene Arms and with the landlady of one of his other locals. I once walked into this particular pub, where George used to play pool, and caught him red-handed, fondling her bum! I was livid. It was all right for George to accuse me of getting up to all sorts behind his back when I didn't so much as look at another man, and there he was copping a feel! But when I confronted him, he had the cheek to deny it, never mind that I had seen it with my own eyes.

I was already starting to feel slightly suspicious about what George was up to when a couple of days later he said, 'Alex, why don't you go out with your girlfriends tonight?' This was completely out of character; George had never made such a suggestion before. Immediately, my suspicions were raised. I agreed and went out but came back unexpectedly an hour later, only to discover

George sitting on the sofa stark naked. He seemed rather surprised to see me and said he was going to bed. A few minutes later there was a rap on the window and I looked out to see the landlady standing outside. As soon as she saw me her face fell, and she muttered something about wanting to see if George was OK.

'He's fine, thanks,' I replied icily, shutting the window briskly and thinking all kinds of dark thoughts about her. With her bleached blonde hair and tarty clothes she had mutton written all over her and she was 56 if she was a day. I marched into the bedroom and demanded to know why she had turned up. George shrugged and said he really didn't know. Like hell you don't, I thought to myself. I was under no illusions about his womanising reputation when I married him. He had a terrible track record. I don't think he had ever actually been faithful to a woman before, but he swore he would never cheat on me. 'Just as well,' I had told him. 'I can put up with a lot but I will never put up with that.'

Later that summer we went away to Portugal with my family and some friends. Once again it was a relief to be away from Chelsea, but George's drinking, which usually calmed down when we went away, grew rapidly worse this time. He was drunk for most of the two weeks. Instead of getting up and going to the Phene, he got up and went and sat at the beach bar – all right, it was a hell of a lot nicer than the pub, but I didn't want to spend my entire holiday in a bar! Every morning we'd come down to the kitchen to discover he'd raided the fridge. He'd get ravenous in the night as the alcohol was wearing off and then eat whatever he could lay his hands on. The cheese would have teeth marks in it, there would be slices of half-eaten watermelon and pieces of half-eaten bread lying around. Back then, tidying up after himself was an alien concept to George.

One morning, around eleven o'clock, we were sitting round the pool and George came outside fully dressed, saying, 'Where are we going for dinner?' He simply had no idea what the time was. I was aware of everyone around me looking at each other in dismay. None of us liked seeing George like this.

I think I was in denial about just how bad his drinking problem was and the effect it was having on me. I tried to blank it out, to pretend things weren't quite as bad as they were, to brush it under the carpet. It was becoming my survival strategy.

Back home, George had plenty of work to keep him occupied; the trouble was, if he didn't want to do it, he wouldn't. He was booked to open The Modern Homes Exhibition in Dublin and we flew out together. However, the following day, when we were due at the exhibition, George was nowhere to be found. I discovered that he had flown back home, leaving me in the highly embarrassing situation of having to open the exhibition in his place! I never particularly enjoyed public speaking at the best of times, never mind having to stand in for my errant husband. I could laugh about this incident later; other incidents were less amusing...

It was half-past eleven one Saturday morning. The phone rang.

'Alex, he isn't here, do you know where he is?' I had a sick feeling in the pit of my stomach. It was the producer from Sky. George hadn't turned up for work. It wasn't the first time, either. Saturdays could sometimes be my sanctuary – the one day of the week when I knew where George was, the one day when he couldn't drink. I'd switch on the TV at midday and see him safely ensconced in the studio, leaving me free to go off and do my own thing. I could catch up with friends, do some shopping and look forward to the evening when we could go out for dinner – the one evening in the week when I could guarantee that George would be sober enough to come because he'd been working all day. Or, like this particular Saturday, it could be hell.

George had obviously decided to go drinking instead of going to work. I had suspected he might go AWOL. He'd been drinking so much lately that he looked really rough, and George was very particular about his appearance. He really didn't like appearing on TV if he didn't look good, and on this particular Saturday he looked awful. With a heavy heart I promised to see if I could track him down. He wasn't at the Phene, so I tried his second bolthole, the pub he would escape to when he really didn't want to be found. There he was, sitting at a table, drinking brandy – never a good sign.

'They've just called me, are you going in? I can give you a lift.'

George shook his head. I saw from the hard look in his eyes that trying to persuade him would be pointless. By now I could tell when he was determined to go on a bender, just from the way he would slick his hair back in the morning, and by the way his normally sparkling eyes turned cold and mean.

Suddenly, the last thing I wanted to do was to go back to the flat and wait for him to come home. Instead, I went out and met my best friend Julie. Laughing with her was a great way of forgetting what George was doing. I needed the release – sometimes the stress of living on Planet George, as I called it, could really get to me. I was actually feeling quite happy as I walked back to the flat. However, as soon as I walked into the hall I was met with an acrid smell of burning.

What the hell's happened now? I thought wearily. George had nearly burned the flat down on more than one occasion when he'd made fry-ups and then fallen asleep with the pan still on the stove. I marched into the kitchen to be confronted by the sight of my beautiful Chanel suit lying in the bin, a hideous burn mark on the jacket. It was ruined. It was such a petty, vindictive thing to do. He knew that I loved that suit; it had been one of my favourite outfits.

When he came home, I flung it at him, shouting, 'What did you do that for?'

Instantly he was enraged and started pushing me around the lounge, shouting at me, even though he was the one completely in the wrong. It was the first time he had pushed me in anger and I was shocked. Unfortunately it wouldn't be the last.

In the morning, he was very contrite. Instead of going to the pub he took me out for lunch and insisted on buying me a pair of boots that he knew I had my eye on. I wanted things to be good between us, so I was only too happy to accept his apology and believed his promise that it wouldn't happen again. And for a while it didn't. We celebrated our second Christmas together and I felt closer to him than ever.

Before I met George he had never really been into Christmas, whereas it's always been a big event for my family; we always get everyone together and lavish presents on each other, as well as stuffing our faces with delicious food and playing endless games of Trivial Pursuit and charades. George was a little sceptical about getting into the spirit of things for our first Christmas, but by our second one he was a convert. We spent it at Mum and Dad's and he loved it. He was like a big kid really, looking forward to handing out all his presents and wanting to win all the games. Then he took us all to Cirque de Soleil, which was to become a Christmas tradition for us after that. At times like these, when he was happy and so loving towards me, I couldn't imagine that anything could ever go wrong between us again. But, as it turned out, it didn't take long before something did. Just a few weeks into the new year, in fact.

29th January 1997, my 25th birthday. I woke up feeling miserable. There was none of that tingle of excitement you sometimes get on your birthday, when you think it's going to be your special day. I'd had a row with George and we weren't speaking – it can't have been over anything important, because I can't even remember what it was about. I lay in bed waiting for him to say 'Happy Birthday' so that we could put the argument behind us and enjoy the day together. But he ignored me, got up and went straight to the pub without saying a word, leaving no card, no present, nothing.

It was too much; I burst into tears. Then I pulled myself together and called Julie. Like the good friend she is, she rushed over and took me out for lunch. I was terribly upset, though, and throughout the day I repeatedly called George at the pub. They kept saying that he wasn't there, but I knew goddamned well he was; they were always covering up for him.

Finally, I went home in despair. I sat in the living room waiting for him to come home, growing more and more angry. As his key turned in the lock I leaped to my feet and as soon as he walked in I screamed, 'How dare you not see me on my birthday!'

Before I knew what was happening, George had punched me in the face. I staggered back in agony, holding my hand to my face, but then he came at me again, violently pushing me. I momentarily cowered and then I fought back, punching and kicking him in self-defence. After a few minutes of frenzied fighting he suddenly ran out of the flat. I staggered to the bathroom, splashed cold water on my face and surveyed the damage – I had a black eye, bruised face and cut neck. 'Happy Birthday' indeed. I curled up in bed weeping, feeling more wretched than I ever had in my life. I couldn't believe that he had done this to me.

The next morning, I called my mum. She came up as soon as she could. I can't imagine how awful it must have been for her seeing her daughter looking so battered and bruised. She was strong for my sake and insisted that I went to the police to have the incident logged. 'Even if you don't press charges you've got to have this on record, because can you imagine if you ended up killing him after a fight?'

It seemed incredible that my mother should be talking about my husband like this, but then I could hardly believe that I was the woman in the mirror with the black eye and split lip.

I gave in to her persuasion, went along to the police station and reported what had happened. I hated doing it, but could see my mum's point of view. The police wanted me to press charges, but I wouldn't. By the time we returned to the flat the press had already been tipped off and were camped outside. Great, that was all I needed. Since our marriage we'd had a low profile in the press but now the story of our bust-up was going to be plastered across the front pages. Unable to face George, I went back to my parents.

They were understandably upset by what had happened, but there was nothing they could do. It was my marriage and I had to sort it out myself – for them to get involved would only make things worse. So when

George called, begging for forgiveness and pleading for me to come home, they didn't say anything when I agreed. But from then on my dad stopped having a drink in the evening, just in case he got an SOS call from me asking him to pick me up.

My friends were also concerned about the way things seemed to be going with my marriage. Some of them would get so angry on my behalf and they'd say, 'You're young, why don't you walk away now? You're wasting all of your twenties with him; you're wasting your life!' But I didn't listen. I still loved him so much I was prepared to accept that this is what my marriage was like – some very good times and some very bad ones. To me, even after he'd hit me, I still believed the good times outweighed the bad. Also, when you're in a relationship with an alcoholic, you start to accept their extreme behaviour as normal. People ask how on earth you can put up with it, but that's what you're used to, that's what you know. It may sound naïve, it may even sound foolish that I stayed with him and put up with the bad times, but I believed he was the love of my life and I couldn't imagine walking away from him.

CHAPTER TEN

CHELSEA BLUES

I had lived in the tiny flat in Oakley Street for nearly two years and apart from the odd touch here and there I hadn't been able to do very much to it at all. Part of the problem was that there was a question mark over who actually owned the flat, something that went back to George's bankruptcy. We really didn't want to spend too much money on it when we didn't know how much longer we'd be living there. But its shabby appearance drove me mad! Ironically, it was after a quarrel with George in April 1997 that I was finally able to embark on some much-needed redecoration.

Now I had taken control of the finances, I was determined that we wouldn't get into debt, so I would give George spending money every day. He simply couldn't be trusted with a credit or debit card, as I knew if he got drunk he wouldn't be able to control his spending. On this particular day in April he had stormed out of the flat after grabbing about £400. He was gone for hours. He had never stayed out all night before and as it was getting later I was growing more and more anxious. I paced round the living room, chain smoking, wondering where on earth he could be.

Finally, at half-past four in the morning, he rolled in.

'Where the hell have you been?' I demanded.

'The casino,' he replied.

'Oh my God, I suppose you've blown all our money?'

'Actually,' he said, 'I've done quite well.'

And I watched in amazement as he started pulling chip after chip from his jacket pockets. Immediately, I started counting them.

'Bloody hell, George,' I said. 'There's over ten thousand pounds here!' We embraced each other, laughing hysterically – the row forgotten.

At last I had my redecorating fund. There was no way I was going to let George blow his winnings. The next day we both went to the Palm Beach Casino in the West End. I gave George £1,000 to gamble with, then cashed in the rest of the chips. As a precaution I got a cheque, which I promptly paid into the bank. Then we treated ourselves to lunch and spent the afternoon in bed, making up for the row and celebrating our good fortune.

The following day I called one of George's friends from The Phene Arms who was a decorator – that was one of the few good things about the pub, it was a great source of skilled tradesmen. If you wanted someone to do something round the house you'd always be able to find them at the Phene. Within a couple of weeks the flat was unrecognisable – out went the grey threadbare carpet, and in came the lovely pale-pink one I ordered; the peeling living-room walls were treated to a new lick of paint. But it was in the bedroom where I really made my mark and created an ultra-feminine boudoir. The hideous embossed wallpaper was replaced by a pretty Laura Ashley design; I put up new metal curtain rods and hung matching Laura Ashley curtains. Now at last the bedroom felt like it belonged to me; no other woman had lain in the bed and looked at those walls!

I decided, somewhat rashly, to paint the kitchen myself. I thought I'd use a bit of artistic licence and planned to give the walls a mottled effect, so I painted them white, then sponged green paint on top. I'd obviously watched one too many home-improvement programmes, where they make everything look so easy, because my walls looked awful – much as if a three-year-old had chucked paint all over them while having a tantrum.

I knew George would be furious, so I dashed off to Homebase to buy more paint to cover up my mistake. But by the time I returned home it was too late, and George was gazing in disbelief at the kitchen.

'What have you done, have you gone mad?' He wasn't smiling; he was genuinely cross with me – or maybe it seemed like the perfect excuse to go back to the pub. He marched off to the Phene in a huff and I stayed up until three in the morning painting over the walls. The following day I added some stencil designs.

This time even George had to admit that it looked really good, so I wasn't such a DIY failure after all!

I was much happier in the flat now that it finally felt more like my home, but it was still far too small and claustrophobic – especially in the summer, when I longed to be able to sit in a garden rather than roast in the living room. Fortunately George's work did take the pair of us away a lot and I discovered that there were definite perks to being Mrs Best. In July 1997 for our second wedding anniversary the *Daily Star* offered to take us to the beautiful island of Mauritius to do an interview and photoshoot about our relationship. The thought of lounging on a beach and staying at a luxury hotel in return for a few hours of our time was too good an offer to turn down. However, yet again George was drinking heavily – for some reason his drinking would always get much worse during the summer – and he was a complete nightmare on the flight over. He kept pestering me to go to the galley and get him another drink, but even then he wouldn't lie back and relax; he played Sixties music on his personal stereo and insisted on singing along loudly to it. Honestly, it would have been easier travelling with a two-year-old! It was such a relief when we finally landed.

The trip wasn't as idyllic as it might have been – for a start it poured with rain every afternoon and we spent a lot of time playing cards with Jeanie Savage, the photographer, and Dawn, who was going to be interviewing us, instead of relaxing in the sun. Also, it was a real struggle waking George up in the morning and getting him to look good for the photographs.

'Alex, I've got some sleeping pills, why don't we try giving George one?' Jeanie finally suggested.

I agreed, and that night we popped one into his drink when he wasn't looking. It definitely did the trick, because the following morning George woke up and said he'd had one of the best nights' sleep of his life. Finally he was ready for his close-up. The trouble was, I was having a hair crisis: all the humidity was making my hair go frizzy and I had to spend hours in the hairdressers getting it straightened. But the photos and interviews only took a day and the rest of the time we were free to relax.

Jeanie's pills had given me an idea. I really couldn't face the thought of a hyperactive George on the flight home, so I slipped a couple of sleeping tablets in his drink an hour into the flight. Within ten minutes he was fast asleep. He didn't even stir when we stopped to re-fuel at Nairobi. He finally came to an hour away from Heathrow, scarcely able to believe he'd slept for so long. I finally confessed what I'd done – a year later. 'You cheeky thing!' was his response.

Every summer, George's son Calum would fly over from the States and stay with us for a couple of weeks. I think I probably treated him more like a younger brother than a stepson, as there were only nine years between us, but on at least one occasion people took us to be a couple. Once when he was fifteen I'd taken him to the doctor, as he had a throat infection. 'Well, said the doctor, 'aren't you lucky to have such a lovely lady looking after you.' Calum and I collapsed in giggles as soon as we walked out of the surgery, but I made him promise not to tell George, as I knew he wouldn't see the funny side to it at all. I'd already had to keep quiet about the Russian gardener who worked for the neighbours. One time I had returned to the flat and he had called out in his halting English, 'Your father has gone out.' I just prayed that he never asked George where his daughter was.

I used to love it when Calum stayed with us because George would make a real effort not to drink and we would go on trips together. He would take us up to see a match at Manchester United or we'd see the sights in London, go to the cinema, or lunch at Langan's. It was lovely doing things together, like a family. But inevitably, after a few days of being superdad, George would gravitate back to the Phene and if Calum wanted to see his dad he'd have to tag along too.

Financially, things were looking much more secure for us towards the end of 1997. George was earning very good money with his after-dinner speeches and television work for Sky. Phil and I had worked hard to rebuild his reputation, and we made sure he didn't just take on any old work. He was a class act and we didn't want him wasting his time in dives for no money. I was even able to start building up a savings account. But both George and I were very anxious about the impending court case over our flat. We knew that if we lost the flat we would be homeless and we'd have great difficulty in getting a mortgage because George had been made bankrupt.

Perhaps this should have brought us closer together, as we both faced the crisis together, but instead George chose to drink to blot out his anxiety and as a result the rows between us escalated – and, with them, George's unreasonable behaviour. He'd storm off to the pub and I would move back to my parents and wait for him to calm down. I ended up having to move out of the flat at least once a week. It was exhausting and emotionally draining and ever since he had destroyed my beautiful Chanel suit I couldn't risk leaving any of my clothes in the flat. As a result I would have to load all my favourite things into bin bags and take them with me. I became like a very upmarket Chelsea bag lady, lugging all my worldly goods with me, and our flat became like a conveyor belt of bin bags – there would always be a row of them in the hall either about to be taken away by me following an argument or about to be packed away following a reconciliation.

Of course, if George couldn't wreak havoc with my clothes after a row, there were other things he could turn his attention to. He was nothing if not resourceful.

That's strange, I thought, as I walked into our bedroom on one occasion, following yet another argument. There's something missing. It was my collection of teddy bears. Both George and I shared a passion for bears and I had a collection of about ten, including one little bear I'd been given when I was christened. For our first Christmas together George had bought me two huge teddies we'd seen in a shop in Manchester. He had actually sent Martin up to buy them and the poor man had to lug the giant bears back to London on a crowded commuter train. I hunted everywhere in the flat but couldn't find them anywhere. Finally I gave up and called George in the Phene. He was drunk and, when I asked him where the bears were, he cryptically replied, 'In a hole,' and put the phone down.

What on earth did he mean? I'd just about given up when my neighbour knocked on my door. 'Do you know anything about those teddy bears in the road outside?'

I looked out of the window. Sure enough, there was a large hole in the road, as the gas board were laying new pipes. I rushed outside and there, lying in the bottom of a deep, dark pit, were my beloved bears. I quickly picked them up and took them back inside. 'They're mine,' I explained to my surprised neighbour. 'I've no idea how they got there, though.' She went upstairs, clearly thinking I was bonkers. I was just relieved she'd seen them, because the next day the gas board sealed the hole and my teddies would have been history.

Then there was the red wine incident. At one of George's after-dinner speeches, the organisers presented me with a lovely bottle of Rothschild Premier Cruz, which couldn't be opened for ten years. When I got back to the flat after yet another row I discovered that George had opened it and poured the lot down the sink in a fit of rage. I'm rather ashamed to admit that I was so enraged by this that, when he returned home, I shouted at him and when he didn't respond I took off my shoe, which had a heavy wooden heel, and threw it at him, hitting him in the face. It was horrible feeling that I was sinking to his level.

I was beginning to get used to George's unpredictable and often erratic behaviour, but I was becoming increasingly disturbed by the way he would resort to violence if we started arguing. I had prayed that his hitting me on my 25th birthday was a one-off, and he had promised that it would never happen again. But it was a promise he couldn't seem to keep. During a row he would inevitably end up pushing me, pulling my hair and slapping me on my face, often hard. At that time I only weighed about six stone, as the stress of living with an alcoholic was obviously getting to me, and it was very frightening when he attacked me. I would end up hitting back in self-defence – I hated doing it, but felt it was a last resort for me.

It was a far cry from what I had imagined married life to be. I know if one of my friends had told me they were being hit I would have told them to leave. But I put up with it, always praying things would get better. Now I would run a mile if a man as much as raised his hand to me – I would never tolerate physical violence against me again. Back then, though, George and I seemed to be locked into a endless cycle of rowing and making up, all connected to his endless cycle of bingeing, and drinking and then not drinking. I excused his behaviour by saying to myself that he was an alcoholic and couldn't help it, which was a stupid excuse for me to use, because that was his excuse too.

When he stopped drinking, even if it was for a few days, he would be lovely, a different person entirely, back to the man I had fallen in love with. We'd get to do things as a couple; we'd go to the cinema, go out to the country for gorgeous walks, see my parents, have dinner with friends. And it would be perfect – until the next time. Sometimes he'd apologise after a major row; sometimes he'd make up in other ways. One time I came back to discover that he had filled the entire flat with flowers – he'd put them in every room, even in the bathroom. And he was always leaving me little love letters, telling me how precious I was to him and how much he loved me.

Sometimes, though, he wouldn't even remember what had happened and I didn't want to keep going on about it, cataloguing what he'd done, as that would only provoke him. When things were fine, I would do everything I could to keep them that way. But I frequently felt as if I was walking eggshells, not wanting to say anything that would set him off because I often felt that George would make an argument out of nothing, to give himself the excuse to go off drinking. I never thought of speaking to anyone about his drinking and getting support for myself. Back then I hadn't heard of the service that Alcoholics Anonymous provides for relatives of alcoholics, but even if I had I probably wouldn't have used it. I couldn't imagine sharing my situation with a roomful of strangers. My mother was my counsellor, when I felt able to tell her what was happening. Otherwise, I kept things to myself.

It was getting so that even when he was sober I could never entirely relax, because I knew that when he started drinking again it would be a big bender that would probably last two weeks. There were so many times when I begged him to cut down his drinking and he promised that he would. I don't think he ever had any intention of doing so – he was just telling me what he knew I wanted to hear. But I was also cautious about having too much of a go at him, because then he would sneak off behind my back and I would rather know where he was. Instead, I tried my best to look after him. When he returned home in the afternoons, paralytic, I would always try and make him have something to eat – anything to soak up the alcohol. I'd make comfort food such as the lasagnes and shepherd's pies that I'd learned to cook since we'd married. But he'd just pick at them. Alcoholics really don't have large appetites.

I'm sure if we had never left Chelsea I would have found George's drinking intolerable, but we were lucky in that he was always getting offers of work that took us abroad, helping him break his drinking habits, if only for a week or so. One such trip was for him to open a betting service for Victor Chandler in Hong Kong. As he owns one of the largest betting empires in the world, we were guaranteed a luxury trip, and we certainly got it – first-class plane tickets and a breathtaking hotel.

'Cheers, Bestie,' I said, clinking my champagne glass against his as we both reclined in one of the largest jacuzzis I had ever seen.

We smiled at each other – this was the life! One entire wall in the fabulous bathroom of the Penninsula Hotel was made of glass, so as we luxuriated in the hot water we could look out over Hong Kong. It certainly beat our tiny bathroom in Chelsea! This was easily one of the most amazing hotels I have ever stayed at. You could actually lie in bed, and press a button to open or shut the curtains – how lazy was that! And the trip couldn't have come at a better time: our court case was only a month away and we were both finding the tension unbearable. George was in a great mood and he did what was expected of him – gave a good speech, shook lots of hands and then we were extravagantly wined and dined.

In May we finally had the court case over the flat. As George and I had feared, we had to give it up and move out, but fortunately we were given quite a large pay-off in compensation, which we'd be able to use towards a new place, so things weren't quite as bleak as we had imagined. I had one week to pack up all our things, get them put into storage and move out of the flat. Martin was a great help; George simply went to the pub. Now we were homeless and had to move in with Mum and Dad. I didn't mind a bit, because at least I would have company. George carried on with his routine, travelling up to London to the Phene – he was nothing if not a creature of habit.

I immediately turned my attention to house-hunting with Victoria, a very good friend of mine who is an estate agent. She found us a beautiful one-bedroomed

A day out at the Celebrity Soccer Six tournament.

Above: With Rod Stewart and Penny Lancaster.

Below: Despite all the activity, there was still time for a cuddle with George up in the commentary box.

At the races in Dubai.

Above: Studying the form.

Below: Enjoying the hospitality with Angie Rutherford.

Above: George placing a charity bet on the FA Cup.

Below: George and I made cameo appearances as ourselves at the end of the film *Best*. My costume was a bit different from my real wedding dress!

Above: George's 54th birthday party at Brian Turner's restaurant. Sitting with us are George's agent, Phil and his partner Kirstin, plus my mum and dad.

Below: George with our dog, Red, looking through the cards sent to him during his stay in hospital.

The move to Northern Ireland was an attempt to make a fresh start and conquer George's illness.

Above: Our new house – that's George collecting the wood.

Below: In the back garden with Red.

Above: In our snooker room in Northern Ireland, with George's dad, Dickie (*right*) and one of his friends. *Inset*: My favourite picture of George – taken by me.

Below: Making a pilot for a cookery programme – sadly, nothing came of it as we moved back to England shortly afterwards.

Happy anniversaries.

Above: Our first anniversary, celebrating at the Palm Beach Casino.

Below: Relaxing on the Orient Express, my surprise trip for our 7th anniversary.

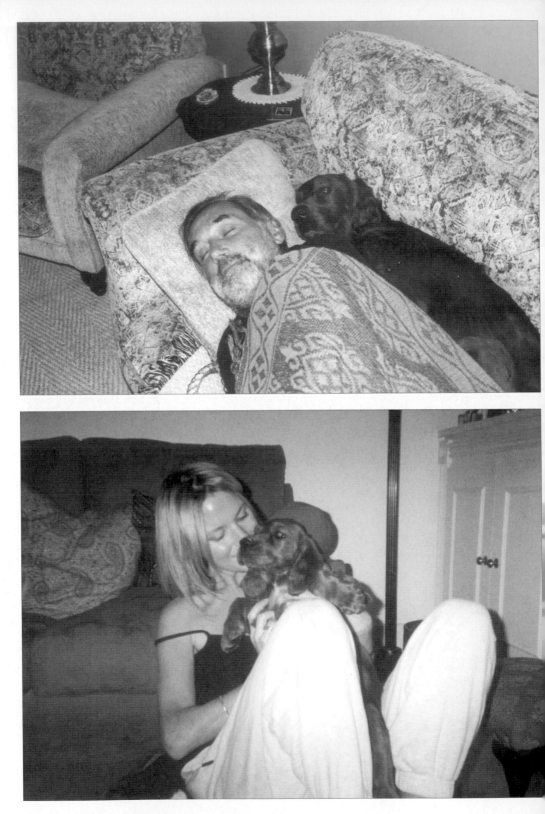

Above: Peace at last.

Below: A dog's life isn't so bad for our Red.

flat I fell in love with instantly on Cheney Walk, two minutes away from where we had lived. All George would have to remember to do when he came out of the Phene would be to turn right instead of turning left, so he liked it too! I put an offer in straight away.

The main difficulty was getting a mortgage offer, because of George's bankruptcy. We were turned down by lots of companies and I was starting to despair that we'd never get a mortgage. We still hadn't lined one up in June, when we were due to go on holiday to Corfu with Mum and Dad and a group of friends. This would be the first time that George had seen the place where I had spent so many happy summers and I had been looking forward to sharing it with him. But on holiday, he was clearly feeling the pressure of not having a home and so spent most of the days drinking in the local tavernas. There would be times when I would have to drive him back from the taverna, then physically drag him down the hill to our villa because it was too steep for a car. Once he was inside, I could relax, as in his inebriated state he was hardly going to be able to climb the hill, and the villa had a cast-iron entrance gate that I locked; he was effectively my prisoner. In between running around after him, I spent hours on the phone trying to sort out our mortgage. Then I heard that someone else had put in an offer on the flat and I was distraught. Just as I had given up hope, however, Victoria put me in touch with a company who finally gave us a mortgage.

By the time we got home, our offer on Cheney Walk

had been accepted. I was elated, and convinced that this flat was the fresh start that George and I needed. I had never entirely felt the old flat belonged to me – I could still feel the ghost of his ex-girlfriend hanging over us. Now we had the chance to make our own home. And I hoped George would feel the same as me. I think deep down he had wondered whether I would stay with him if he was homeless; even after nearly three years together I think he thought I might leave him if he lost the flat in the court case.

I went mad in the summer sales, buying sofas and tables, rugs and curtains. The flat had recently been redecorated and was lovely, with stripped wooden floors, and pristine white walls. There was a large reception room, a double bedroom with an ensuite bathroom and best of all a big kitchen. Finally I could fit a dining table and chairs in and – joy of joys – a washing machine! No more hand-washing my knickers in the sink! I could make the kitchen into my den and, if George was watching the football in the lounge, I could retreat into the kitchen to watch my soaps on a portable. And I loved the fact that there was a patio – admittedly it was tiny, but I craved some outside space.

Within a couple of months we had moved in. Mum and Dad helped me on moving day. George returned from the pub in the afternoon to find everything in place; he literally hadn't had to lift a finger. I didn't mind; I wanted him to be happy. If he was happy, so was I.

For a while, things were much better. We adored our new home and George seemed as if a weight had been lifted from his shoulders. Now we were the proud owners of a dining table, we could entertain, and both of us loved having friends round for dinner. Every Sunday I would cook a huge roast and invite round all George's friends from the Phene to have lunch with us.

Now we had a home of our own and were settled at last, we decided to start trying for a baby. I've always wanted to have children and there didn't seem to be any reason to delay any longer. Secretly, I hoped that if we had the child we longed for George might finally be able to beat his addiction – even though I knew he hadn't been able to the first time he became a father. He certainly didn't seem to be making any effort to cut down as we tried, though – even though excessive alcohol can affect fertility.

Unfortunately, the euphoria of getting our new home didn't last long for George, and the final months of 1998 and the whole of 1999 would turn out to be some of the worst times of my marriage. George should have been happy, he had plenty of work coming in, but it wasn't enough to keep him from drinking. It wasn't as if he was content just getting quietly drunk, either. Quite often he would end up getting into scrapes in the pubs and come to blows. I'm sure people would goad him into it: they would pester him and wind him up so they could boast that they'd had a fight with George Best. In the same way, so many people seemed to delight in buying him a drink, just so they could say they had. Well, weren't they big men, buying a drink for an alcoholic?

One evening I witnessed a horrible fight that broke out around George. It was a rare occasion when I had decided to go with him to The Beehive, another of his locals, and equally as shabby as the Phene. He was playing pool and I was just putting some music on the jukebox in the lounge when I heard a massive commotion and a scream. I rushed into the pool room to be confronted by the shocking sight of a man lying on his back, with one eye pouring with blood – someone had just thrust a snooker cue into his eye. I'd had first-aid training, and quickly took charge. I knew that if one eye is injured you have to cover the other one straight away. Thankfully, the man didn't lose his eye, but he was lucky. George later said he hadn't seen what had happened, but the whole episode made me wish he didn't feel the need to go to such rough pubs – it was as though he had a hidden radar to find the most unpleasant dive and hang out in it.

Then the rows between us started up again. Sometimes I could laugh about them. Take the instance when George returned from the pub, and instead of cooking dinner, as I usually did, I had ordered in a take-away curry. I can't remember what triggered the row, but before I knew it George had lobbed his chicken curry straight at me. I managed to step out of the way and the food ended up splattered on our beautiful white walls. Furiously, I pelted my onion bhajis at George's head. He retaliated with rice, so I hit back by throwing my chicken curry at him. We made the most tremendous mess, so bad that we had to have the living room redecorated. The turmeric in the curry had stained the walls yellow. I was mortified when our decorator friend from the Phene, who turned up to repaint the walls, asked me what had happened.

I am quite a resilient person, so instead of brooding after a quarrel I made sure I did something that made me happy. I'd see my friends or go shopping. Browsing through the shops soothed me, and when I found some lovely item of clothing it took some of the sting out of the argument – that is, if the row hadn't been too serious. In fact, I was building up quite a wardrobe, given the number of arguments we'd been having lately! In the summer, I made a spectacular purchase following a row. After George had done his usual disappearing act to the pub, I marched off to a BMW showroom, where I ended up buying a BMW convertible. Well, I reasoned, it's the summer, it will be good having the roof down. Besides, it's for both of us – even though George had lost his licence some years earlier and so actually it would be me who would have the pleasure. It might sound excessive, but I needed to do things like that to keep my sanity.

Following one particularly nasty row, George stormed out, saying that he wanted a divorce. I didn't pay too much attention; he was, as usual, drunk. I still felt upset, though. Suddenly I heard the front door opening. It couldn't be George; I wasn't expecting him back for ages. I was stunned to see one of the locals from the Phene, who just happened to be a locksmith, standing in the hallway, holding my keys. He looked equally shocked to see me.

'Oh, Alex,' he stuttered, 'I didn't think you'd be here.'

'Where did you think I'd be? This is my house!' I said.

'Well, George has just told me you've split up and he asked me to come round and change the locks.'

I was livid. I demanded he hand me the set of keys and sent him away with a flea in his ear. I had hoped that the rows would ease off now we were settled, but I was deluding myself. They seemed to get worse, and after one nasty argument that escalated into a physical fight I ended up in hospital with a broken arm. George pushed me violently and I fell over awkwardly and hit my arm on the floor. Instantly, I knew I'd broken it – it was the same arm I'd broken when I was thirteen. He left before I could tell him what had happened, so I had to get myself to Chelsea and Westminster casualty. I was there all night. When I finally got home at six in the morning George had the nerve to shout at me, 'Where the hell have you been?'

'Look at my plaster cast, where do you think I've been!'

It would have been funny, if it hadn't been so awful. He was shocked about what he had done to me and begged me to forgive him. He was honest enough to tell people what had happened, but I think he felt deeply ashamed and embarrassed. I knew he hadn't meant to cause me to break my arm, but I felt very upset all the same. As usual I put on a brave face and tried to make the best of things. The only good thing to come of it was that I had the excuse to have my hair washed and blow-dried at the hairdressers twice a week – a real indulgence, which I carried on for quite a while, even when my arm was out of plaster. Well, I told myself, I think I deserve a little treat!

December 1998. I was looking forward to Christmas. It would be our first one in our new flat and I wanted everything to be perfect. I loved decorating the tree, which George and I had chosen together, and putting decorations round the flat. Christmas had always been such a special time for my family and me and I really wanted George to share in the festivities. But his drinking was out of control. I'd been Christmas shopping in Harrods and thought I'd pop in on George at the pub on my way home. When I walked in, though, he wasn't there. The locals looked very shifty when I asked where he was; they were always covering up for him. I kept on at them, however, and finally they admitted that George had been in a fight and had received a nasty cut to his head. Apparently, he had refused to go to hospital and had staggered home instead. I rushed back to the flat. George was lying on the sofa. When he saw me he tried to get up, but fell over. Blood was pouring from the cut.

'Oh my God, George, look at the state of you!'

I realised that I couldn't get him to casualty myself, so in desperation I called an ambulance, explaining that it wasn't an emergency but that there was no other way I could get my husband to the hospital. Fortunately, the paramedics came. In casualty he had to have a number of stitches. I wanted him to rest in bed, but, as soon as we got home, he went straight back to the pub. We spent Christmas Day at my parents'; then I had the whole family over to the flat on Boxing Day. George was drunk the whole time. I wasn't looking forward to 1999.

Early in the new year I had an appointment with a leading fertility expert. George and I had been trying for children for the previous six months and I was anxious to find out if there was any reason why we weren't being successful. An endoscopy revealed that my fallopian tubes were blocked and I would need an operation before I could have any hope of conceiving. I was booked in a few days before my birthday. George was still drinking heavily and so didn't accompany me to the hospital. Fortunately, though, he wasn't too out of it when he received an urgent phone call from the hospital. Luckily, we had given them the phone number of the Phene – as that, of course, is where George was. They were in the middle of performing surgery on me and were phoning to ask George for his consent to remove my fallopian tubes. They had discovered they were in a far worse state than they had realised, but told George that even if they were removed, I should still be able to conceive through IVF. Thank goodness George had the sense to say no. I would never have wanted such drastic action to be taken, as I know that the success rate of IVF is very small. I wanted to give it my best chance of trying to conceive naturally before I had any intervention and George knew this. He came and picked me up in the evening, bearing a huge bouquet and a teddy bear and I told him he had made the right decision.

Apart from this moment of lucidity, though, George seemed hellbent on self-destruction. He started drinking brandy as well as wine. At night I'd have a bottle of Evian by the bed; George would wake up and take swigs from a bottle of Pinot Grigiot. At times he would look terrible, the skin on his face was blotchy and red, his nose was covered in scabs and he had cirrhosis all over his hands – a sure sign that all was not well with his liver.

'I'm sure it won't always be like this,' I'd tell myself. 'I love him and he loves me, and that's what matters.' It wasn't always easy to hang on to that feeling when I saw what drink did to my husband, though. I was walking back to our flat once and suddenly I saw George collapse in a drunken heap in front of me on the street. He looked a pitiful sight in his scruffy old tracksuit, reeking of drink. There were builders working across the road and for a fleeting second I imagined walking past George and pretending I didn't know him. It seemed so embarrassing having to deal with him in this state and so humiliating for him – not that he seemed to care. In the end I managed to pick him up, and drag him home, trying my best to ignore the curious looks from the builders. Back home all I could do was put him to bed, something I was getting used to doing.

In the past, whenever he stopped drinking he seemed to be able to make a quick recovery and would look twenty years younger. Now, increasingly, he looked ravaged by alcohol. He had never been one for going to the doctors, but I was desperate for him to see someone. When we'd taken out life insurance for our new flat, he'd had a medical and was told that his blood tests were worrying and that he really should stop drinking and see a doctor. Of course, he didn't. I was so fearful that he would have a heart attack, like his mother. I couldn't believe that his body could cope with the amount he drank.

He was sick every morning, even on the days he didn't drink. And if he wasn't drinking he'd have the shakes really badly. He was permanently exhausted. It was torture seeing him like this. I begged him to do something about it: 'You're killing yourself,' I cried. But he wouldn't listen. It was the worst time; I was desperately worried about him and felt increasingly isolated and lonely.

A film was being made based on his life, called *Best*, directed by and starring John Lynch, and starring Patsy Kensit as Angie and me – I suppose they were making a point about his liking for similar-looking blondes. George and I were to play ourselves at the end of the film, getting married again. On the morning of the filming, however, George was violently sick. We weren't able to film our piece until much later in the day, and even then he looked terrible. There was something seriously wrong with him, but trying to tell him that was like banging my head against a brick wall.

And the rows continued – the same old same old: George accusing me of flirting. Or he wouldn't turn up for one of his jobs, feel guilty about it and take it out on me. Or he would think that I wasn't speaking to him because of something he'd done. I was being emotionally worn down by it all. I ended up in casualty again after yet another fight, during which George had pushed me. This time I cut my chin so badly I needed six stitches.

I never saw myself as a battered wife. I blamed George's behaviour on the booze. I knew he didn't mean to hurt me, but I was beginning to feel that I couldn't take any more. I couldn't see how we could go on like this; I couldn't see any sign that he was ever going to stop drinking. I started to think that I might have to leave him.

'Happy New Year, darling!' My best friend Julie flung her arms around me and kissed me. I could barely say the same back to her; my eyes were hot with tears and I felt desolate. I was holding a millennium party at our flat and George had barely bothered to make an appearance; he'd turned up late, and then left halfway through to go back to his beloved pub. So he didn't even stay to wish me Happy New Year. What kind of marriage was this? I was sick of coming second best to drink.

He finally staggered back as I was clearing up.

'Thanks a lot,' I shouted at him. 'I made such an effort tonight for the party and all you can do is go and sit in that bloody pub!'

Immediately he flew into a rage, shouting and ranting at me. Then, with grim predictability, he started hitting me, but this time it was harder and more brutal than before. He yanked my hair and then punched me violently in the face. I crumpled to the floor. I thought for one awful moment he had broken my jaw.

It was the start of a new year, but I felt as if I had nothing to look forward to. I just can't go on like this, I thought over and over, as I lay in bed crying. In the morning my dad called round to collect something. He took one look at my swollen, battered face and then exploded, 'How dare you do this to my daughter?'

George mumbled something about being really sorry and, predictably, left the flat.

I very nearly left him after that attack, but in the weeks that followed George was becoming more and more unwell and I was desperately worried about him. Even after all he had put me through, I felt I couldn't abandon him.

CHAPTER ELEVEN

IN SICKNESS AND IN HEALTH

'Alex, look at this, it won't stop bleeding.'

I walked into the bathroom. George was frantically trying to stop the flow of blood streaming down his leg.

'It was a scab, I just knocked it.'

I tried to hide my concern and help George staunch the blood. By then I was so anxious about his deteriorating health that I was reading up on liver problems and I knew that one of the symptoms of liver failure was thinning of the blood and its inability to clot.

God, George, I thought, what have you done to yourself?

Our February visit to the health farm didn't seem to be doing George any good at all. He was still being violently sick every morning, but he refused to do anything about it. Back at the flat, in desperation I started giving him milk thistle, a herbal remedy that is supposed to be good for the liver, and I bought a recipe book about cooking for people with liver problems. I even tried to get George to eat dandelion leaves and molasses, which were recommended in the book, but, frankly, getting him to eat anything was impossible – he had no appetite at all. And, even though he had promised once and for all to stop drinking, he would still drag himself off to the Phene. He swore that he wasn't drinking brandy any more, that it was just white wine spritzers, but I didn't believe him.

In mid-February George had agreed to speak at a university in Ireland. By now he couldn't even walk properly; his face was starting to turn yellow, as were the whites of his eyes, and he kept being sick. Somehow he managed to make the speech, but back at the hotel he collapsed into bed, while I lay beside him crying. Even after all he had put me through, I still loved him. All I wanted was for him to be well.

'Alex, you've got to get him to see a doctor,' Mum said urgently to me as we sat round the dinner table. We'd gone round to my parents for the evening, but George had felt so ill that he'd had to go to bed.

'He looks terrible,' my mum said again.

'Of course he needs to see a doctor!' I cried. 'But how am I going to get him there? He refuses to go.'

I didn't know what to do, but every day George seemed to get sicker. He was so unwell that I was seriously starting to think that he might die. I begged him to do something; it was tearing me apart watching him destroying himself and feeling powerless to do anything about it.

Finally, even he couldn't ignore the damage he was doing to himself. A few days after our visit to Mum and Dad, I woke up to hear George groaning in agony next to me. He was clutching his stomach, which was so distended he looked nine months pregnant. Straight away I called an ambulance. George was in such pain that for once he didn't protest.

At Chelsea and Westminster Hospital, the doctors did a series of blood tests. Even though George could barely move, I was still so worried that he'd do a runner that I hid his trainers while we were waiting for the results. The doctors came back with very bad news – the tests showed that his liver was failing. They told him that he was so seriously ill that he would need to be admitted there and then. But George wouldn't hear of it and insisted on returning home.

I was beside myself.

'You've got to go to hospital,' I begged. 'I don't want to be a widow at twenty-eight! Please, George!'

But, even though he was desperately ill, I still don't think he wanted to stop drinking – that way, he wouldn't have to admit how serious his condition was. I didn't know what to do. Could I walk away and let him get on with killing himself? I certainly knew I couldn't bear to sit back and do nothing any longer.

I thought that maybe if I could find a hospital close to us he might consider staying and getting treatment. I phoned the Lister Hospital and spoke to a lovely woman there, who listened to my problem and told me to give her twenty minutes while she found out where George needed to go.

She was true to her word and called back to tell me that the person we needed to see was Professor Williams at the Cromwell Hospital. He was the leading expert in treating liver problems and had performed the first liver transplant in the 1960s. That was the man for us. I called his office at once and made an appointment for George for the following week, the earliest spot they had. I was dreading George's reaction, but he must have been starting to accept that he was dangerously ill, because he agreed – on the condition that he could drink all week.

On 8 March, I practically frog-marched him to the appointment. Professor Williams took one look at him and said, 'Your room is waiting for you.' By then George felt so ill that he simply surrendered.

It was such a relief that he was finally in hospital, though I felt quite overwhelmed with the stress and worry of it all. But now I had to be stronger than ever. I tried to hold back the tears and busied myself with the practicalities of George's stay in hospital, dashing to Marks & Spencer to buy him pyjamas and wash things. Later, when he felt slightly better, he was mortified to discover that I'd bought him three identical pairs, telling me that the nurses would think he never changed them.

George looked sicker than ever in hospital. Straight away, they started pumping drugs into him trying to avert his liver failure. I could hardly believe that the man lying in bed, surrounded by drips and looking so frail, was my husband. By now, because he hadn't been eating properly for the last three weeks, he only weighed around ten and half stone – usually he weighed thirteen.

Within a day the press got hold of the news. Phil called as I was about to go and visit George to warn me that the media were camped outside, and insisted on picking me up. It was hell battling our way through the photographers and journalists to see George – and, needless to say, it was the last thing I needed. They were nothing if not persistent, though, and from then on I was bombarded with phone calls and had journalists ringing my doorbell. I even had Martin Bashir writing me letters, desperate to interview us. It was an extra stress. Every day I had cameras going off in my face, so I'd have to make an effort to put make-up on and look presentable even though I didn't feel like it, as I didn't want to see pictures of myself looking rough! Phil and I took to sneaking in through the side entrance and walking through the Well Woman Clinic, which Phil found highly embarrassing, but I couldn't face seeing the press every day.

George was in hospital for the next eight weeks and so was I, because I spent every day with him. He wanted me there beside him and I wanted to be with him, but it was exhausting and often monotonous. The days can seem very long when you're sitting in the same room – even though George's room rapidly came to resemble a florist, with the number of bouquets sent to him by friends and fans and the number of cards and letters he received. He was chuffed to get a bouquet from Oasis's Gallagher brothers, but rather less impressed with the bunch of white lilies John Scales sent him. 'Is this a hint?' he said to me when they arrived, though he smiled about it later. And he did get plenty of visits from his close friends, including Parky, Milan Mandric from Portsmouth FC and Mohamed Al Fayed, which took some of the burden off me.

I'd be with him by half-past ten every morning, after I'd shopped for things to keep him entertained – newspapers, crossword puzzles and snacks. He developed a craving for Calypo lollies and I had to scour the shops to find him different flavours. Then he'd get an obsession for wine gums and I had to remember to get those. Even though the Cromwell Hospital was private, and so offered a pretty good menu, George still grew tired of the food and so I would have to bring in treats such as roast chicken and salads from Waitrose, or I would make him meals. One night I stayed up until two in the morning making him a key-lime pie! I think the next day I was slightly late going in and George tapped his watch and said, 'And where have you been?' But it was said in jest. Luckily for George, he has many friends in the restaurant trade and he was thrilled when a friend of ours, Michael, the maître d' from Scalinis, brought in feasts for him; on one occasion he even brought in lobster. It was such a joy to see George eating again.

I was starting to feel more optimistic about George's condition, although I was under no illusions. I had become a bit of a walking encyclopaedia on the liver and knew that he had destroyed a very large chunk of his, probably in the region of 75 per cent. The liver is one of the most important organs in the body, responsible for so many vital functions. But it can rejuvenate. I prayed George's could.

Although it was physically and emotionally tiring being around someone who was so sick, I didn't resent it for a second. George was a very good patient; even though he felt very ill, he always put on a brave face. And he was so appreciative and loving towards me. It seemed ironic that he had to be nearly dying for our marriage to be saved. The doctors laid it on the line for him, making it clear that he must never drink again. They told him that his liver might recover, or it might not, and that if it didn't he would need a transplant.

After two long months, the doctors agreed that George could come home. We were delighted. Now there was just the small problem of how to get to him out of the hospital without being photographed. By then we had signed an exclusive deal with a Sunday newspaper for an interview, and weren't allowed to talk to anyone else. In the end we simply walked out of the back door, the one entrance the press weren't covering, and managed to get home without being snapped.

We had whiled away some of the many hours in hospital fantasising about where we could go on holiday when George was discharged, but when he first came home he was simply too weak to do anything and was still having to see Professor Williams every other day. The slightest physical exertion exhausted him and he had to spend a lot of time resting in bed. I was basically his nurse, responsible for administering the many drugs he was on. But I can honestly say that I loved looking after him. I didn't mind what I had to do, or how much time I had to devote to him; I just wanted him to get better. He was back to being the fantastic man I had first fallen in love with – except even better, because now he wasn't drinking.

And, joy of joys, I could finally get rid of the tracksuits that he had been wearing for the previous three years! I had loathed them and they had been a hideous symbol of his drinking days. He had about ten pairs and he always wore them to the pub. If I could have had a ceremonial burning of them, I would have, but the patio was too small. Instead, I binned some, glad that I would never have to set eyes on them again. The others I gave to my mum to give to a charity shop – and, hilariously, when I was driving George along Cheam High Street one day he spotted one of them in a charity shop window. 'That looks familiar, Alex, it's not mine, is it? There was nothing wrong with it.' George looked at me quizzically, but I kept a straight face and replied, 'Of course not!'

The shadow of George's drinking still hung over us, though. We talked about it and he admitted that he would really miss it, but he said he knew those days were over. Now there was the very real problem of how to keep him occupied. It was clear that, even when he was recovered, he couldn't possibly go back to giving his after-dinner speeches as there would be too many temptations to drink. Sky TV had promised to take him back as soon as he was well enough, but that still left a big gap in his diary. A few years earlier I had come up with what I thought was the perfect pastime for him – golf. Phil had even bought him a set of clubs for Christmas, but he had never used them. Jokingly, he had said he couldn't play a sport in which he had to give up possession of the ball!

'I'd like a dog,' he finally said one day, after we'd been to the pictures together. I've always loved dogs, but I knew that Chelsea wasn't an ideal location for one. I also knew that I would end up walking it and looking after it! Then I thought, If that's going to make him happy we'll get one. So I checked out breeders and one afternoon we went to look at some red setters. We came home an hour later with a new puppy, named Red. He was a bit of an impulse purchase, and we didn't have anything for him when we got home – no bed, no toys. But the look on George's face told me I had made the right decision.

Although George was ill, it felt as though we had begun a new chapter in our marriage. I had been on the verge of leaving him, but now it felt like we had the chance to start again.

Just before George's 54th birthday, in May 2000, the Professor gave George permission to go away and I booked a long weekend in Venice as a treat. This was somewhere we had always wanted to go and we had the most romantic time, talking over long lunches, wandering round the galleries and churches and, naturally, being rowed around the canals on a gondola. It was like falling in love again. We had been through so much together that we felt incredibly close. Of course, there was no white heat of physical passion – that would have to reignite when George was better – but I had my soul mate back, my love.

The following month we had our usual big family holiday to Corfu, but poor George felt very unwell. His feet swelled up terribly because of the medication he was on and he was in agony. The only relief he could get was if we wrapped his feet in towels that we'd cooled in the freezer and then he sat with them in buckets of ice. He couldn't do anything except lie on the sofa. He didn't complain – he wanted us all to have a good holiday. The strain of being with a near invalid the whole time was starting to get to me, though. He'd been ill now for four months and I had been with him constantly, giving him my undivided attention, catering for his every need. I never had any time for myself and in Chelsea we had hardly been out or seen anyone. He would go to bed early and I'd be left watching TV on my own. George would tell me to go out and see my friends, but I could tell he didn't really want me to and I didn't want to leave him on his own. It was a strain, though. The night before we were due to fly home I turned round and said in exasperation, 'God, do you always have to be ill!' I really didn't mean it nastily, but George obviously took it to heart because when we landed at Gatwick he took off on his own back to Chelsea, leaving me to struggle with all our luggage.

Back home, George had made a momentous decision. He told me that he didn't want to live in Chelsea, or indeed London, any more. He had decided that he needed to escape from his old haunts and temptations. I adored living in Chelsea, but I understood George's need to get away and so instantly started house-hunting. I quickly found a place in Surrey that I thought would be perfect. George saw it too, agreed that it looked ideal and we put an offer on it. I had set my heart on moving there. I knew I would miss London, but I love the countryside and thought it would help George and me to rebuild a new life. Then, out of the blue, one night he said simply, 'I don't want to live there.'

I was stunned. 'Why not? It's perfect for us.'

He shook his head. 'I don't want to.'

'You can't just change your mind like that,' I answered, 'we'd both agreed.' But at that, he flew off the handle and stormed out of the flat.

I was beside myself with worry. George really wasn't well enough to go off anywhere on his own and I dreaded to think what he was doing. The hours went by and there was still no sign of him. In the early hours of the morning I was startled by the phone ringing. It was a friend of George's from Manchester, calling to see if he was all right because he'd just got a call from

159

the *Manchester Evening News* saying that George had been found lying on a park bench clutching a bottle of champagne.

'Please don't let it be true,' I prayed. Then, large as life, and hopelessly drunk, George walked in, holding the bottle of champagne. Shocked as I was, I didn't have a go at him. George was too out of it to care about the worry he'd caused me and went straight to bed. In the morning he apologised for putting me through such an anxious night, but denied that he'd been found drunk on a park bench. As he'd walked in with the champagne bottle, I found it hard to believe him, though. I tried raising the subject of our move again, but he was adamant that he didn't want to go to Surrey. My dream house would have to be abandoned.

Meanwhile, the press had a field day. We had booked a trip to Marbella, and we were to fly there the next day. We'd barely been back from Corfu but George needed a change of scenery to keep his mind off drinking. But it wasn't going to be a peaceful break. We were pursued by the press at Gatwick and they were waiting for us when we landed. I felt harassed and became furious. Why can't you just leave him alone, I thought to myself, he's having a very difficult time trying to cope with not drinking and this added pressure isn't helping.

We were staying at a friend's apartment, on the top storey with a roof terrace, and from our vantage point we could see the press staking us out on the street below. Luckily, they couldn't see us. It was clearly impossible for us to go to the beach without being pursued, so we spent our days sunbathing on the terrace and only ventured out at night because by then the press had given up, as they couldn't put us in the next day's papers.

One disastrous trip out during the day did make the papers. George was waiting for me in a café and he ordered a glass of wine for me. I didn't even want to have a drink, but ended up being photographed and depicted as some kind of evil cow for drinking in front of my alcoholic husband. It was a horrible feeling being hunted like this. We had never attracted this level of press attention before and it was very disturbing; we felt like prisoners. One paper even printed a mocked-up wanted poster with George's face on it, for pub landlords to stick on their walls as a warning not to serve him.

We both felt under pressure. Back in London, George found it impossible to stay put and said he wanted to go away again, but I really didn't want to. He was then offered a job in Ireland by a so-called friend of his. I had always felt that this man abused his friendship with George, using him for his name and never paying him enough for the work he did for him. 'Don't do it,' I pleaded. 'You're still not well enough.'

By the time I'd returned from walking Red, though, George had packed his bags and gone off to Ireland, without so much as a goodbye. I was livid that he would behave like this and also dreaded that he might have fallen off the wagon again. He might say time and again that he wasn't going to drink any more, but the craving was obviously too strong.

He didn't call me for three days. I heard from his dad, who had seen George and assured me that he seemed to be sober. Well, thanks for phoning me, I thought to myself. One morning, as I was taking Red for a walk, I ended up in Park Lane at a Range Rover showroom. I had only intended to look at the cars, but impulsively I asked to take one on a test drive. Red had to come too – and I'm sure the salesman was delighted by the dog hairs in the back! When I returned from my spin round Hyde Park, I simply said, 'I'll take it.' We needed a bigger car now we had the dog. Besides, it was a good way – albeit an expensive one – of handling the stress of George going AWOL.

Finally, he called. He said he was sorry and that he was coming home. Then he dropped his bombshell. He said that he wanted to live in Ireland in a caravan by the beach and buy a Harley-Davidson. For a moment or two I was speechless. Then I said, 'I'll move to Ireland, if that's what you really want. But I'm definitely not living in a caravan!'

A week later we were both in Ireland, house-hunting. It would be a huge change for me, but I loved him so much that I would have done anything to see him happy. Well, anything except live in a caravan!

CHAPTER TWELVE

ESCAPE FROM LONDON

I looked out of my living-room window, across the field to the sea beyond. It was a stunning view, but as I gazed at it I shivered. It felt so remote. Finally it seemed that George and I had our dream house, but even as we had been signing the completion documents I was worried by how isolated it was. We were moving to a tiny fishing village called Portavogie, in County Down, Northern Ireland. For a girl who was used to the buzz of the King's Road – the shops, the bars and the cafés – it was a big adjustment. The village didn't even have a shop; my nearest supermarket was an hour and a half away. I had only agreed to the move on the condition we kept on our Chelsea flat, so that we would divide our time between London and Ireland. I still had to feel that I had my home in England, close to my friends and family, because here in Northern Ireland I didn't know anybody apart from George's family.

I did love the house, though, and couldn't wait to start putting my mark on it. We had seen it on a day when I'd almost given up hope of finding the right place. We'd driven by this large house standing on its own plot of land by the sea, with a 'For Sale' sign in the front. 'That looks more like it,' I said to George and immediately stopped the car. We hadn't made an appointment, so we just knocked on the door and the owners, an elderly man and his son, were happy to show us round – doubly happy because they had answered the door to George, in fact!

The decor – floral wallpaper and floral carpets – wasn't really to our taste, but the house had four large bedrooms, a conservatory, a huge kitchen, a dining room, a drawing room and a living room. After living in a one-bedroomed flat, the space seemed vast. We put an offer in there and then.

The sale went through very quickly and by October we were ready to complete. When we picked up the keys we raised the matter of the land in front of the house. There were several acres and we thought it would be good to own them as well. The owner said, 'I'll give you the land, but I want money for it.'

'Fine,' replied George, 'how much?'

'A pound!' replied the man. It was so sweet of him and seemed like a good omen for our new home.

At this time George was still very weak and still quite yellow from the jaundice. One night we went to a rugby match and I overheard two spectators in front of us say,

'Have you seen George Best? He looks like one of the walking dead.' I looked anxiously at George, praying he hadn't heard them. But it was true – he did look very ill. When it came to organising the move and getting all the basics in the house sorted out, it was down to me. We had this massive house and absolutely nothing to put in it! I had to buy everything: cutlery, crockery, bedding, furniture, TVs – the lot. My parents were brilliant as usual, and came over and helped me. It was great to have their company, as George was feeling so poorly that he was going to bed by eight o'clock at night.

'Are you sure you're going to be OK stuck out here?' Mum asked me anxiously, when George was safely tucked up.

'Of course, I'll be fine,' I replied breezily, not realising that George wanted us to move here full time. 'This is just a country home.'

I sounded more confident than I felt; I did worry about the isolation. That said, for the first time in our marriage, George was showing an interest in creating a home. We decided to strip everything out and start from scratch. It was going to be our project. Together we pored over colour charts, looked at carpets and chose curtains. I wanted to go for a rustic, old-fashioned look and George agreed.

We spent the next few months travelling all over Ireland, buying furniture and picking up pieces from antique shops. I discovered that George had great taste – his new-found interest in decorating and interior design was a revelation, as he had never shown the slightest interest in the subject before. And it was wonderful spending time together. We'd shop like mad, then treat ourselves to a leisurely lunch and then set off for more retail therapy. At the end of the day we'd get out of the car saying, 'Good shop, good shop!' and unload our many purchases.

Our marriage, which had so far been characterised by endless rows and reconciliations – all the result of George's drinking – was now calm and stable. We could talk about everything and, if we didn't agree about something, George didn't fly off the handle, we'd discuss it. He was a changed man, a trustworthy, loving husband, all that I could ask for. Whenever he was interviewed he would say how much he appreciated me standing by him and I would say to him, 'I'm your wife, that's what marriage is about, staying with someone, in sickness and in health.' We even started to talk about having children again – though we had to be realistic: the medication George was taking would adversely affect his fertility. But it definitely seemed more of a possibility now he wasn't drinking.

The house was quickly transformed. The locals were incredibly keen to help us and I would get calls regularly from tradesmen offering their services. I was especially pleased with my kitchen. We got someone in to lay slate floors and granite work surfaces and it looked fabulous. Everyone was very friendly, but we did feel rather like outsiders. In fact, George's sister Carol had lived in Portavogie for thirty years and she was still classed as an outsider by the locals! But on the whole everyone was delighted George was living on their doorstep. A bit too pleased in some instances...

Unfortunately, when we had moved, one of the Irish newspapers had photographed us and printed our address. On one memorable occasion I opened the door and there was a bus full of elderly ladies who had come on a sight-seeing tour to meet George – their hero. I had to politely tell them that he was ill in bed. In Chelsea everyone was used to seeing famous people and no one batted an eyelid, but George is like the prodigal son in Ireland and everyone wanted to see him. Practically every day I would have people knocking on the door asking for his autograph. Worst of all were the priests. They weren't interested in autographs, but rather in saving George's soul from the demon drink. They would invariably knock on the door when I was in the middle of cooking tea and start preaching away. It was rather disconcerting hearing about hell and damnation when you're worried about your lasagne burning. I'd often have to deal with six of them a day!

Something had to be done, and I invested in a set of wrought-iron gates to go at the bottom of the drive. As an extra deterrent I chose the largest, spikiest pair and put up a large sign saying 'Private'. It didn't make a great difference, though and the priests still managed to get through.

By the end of October George had started working at Sky again and we'd both fly over to London at the weekends. It was blissful not having the stomach-churning anxiety that he wasn't going to turn up for work and it gave me a great opportunity to see my parents and friends and indulge in some retail therapy. This set-up suited me – I could get through the weeks in Ireland knowing that I had my London life to come back to. I needed to have these breaks away, because the weather was making the weeks seem longer and longer. It was unbelievably cold and windy. In December, my friend Julie came over for a visit. We had a great time showing her the house and George treated us to lovely meals out. When I drove Julie to the airport along the coast road the weather was atrocious – the waves were almost reaching the car. As I dropped her off, I did feel a pang of jealousy that she was returning to civilisation and I was stuck in the middle of nowhere. She actually told me that she didn't know how I could live there – and sometimes I didn't either. Back home, George was already in bed and as I sat by the fire listening to the wind howling round the house, I longed to be back in London. I loved our home, but I felt so cut off. Not long till next weekend, I told myself.

Then, at Christmas, George declared that he wanted to move over to Ireland permanently. We were to rent out our London flat and take Red, our dog, back with us; my parents had been looking after him until now. It was a blow. If Red came back with us I wouldn't easily be able to fly between London and Ireland. I would never take him on a plane, as I thought it too cruel, so that would mean a gruelling six-hour car journey and ferry ride to make the trip.

We spent Christmas at my parents', and I was dreading our return home. I knew there was no point in telling George how I felt; he had made up his mind and nothing I said would change it. I was in tears most of the way on the long journey back to Ireland. By now the house was almost finished – how was I going to fill my time?

I had met some more people and now had several very good friends, including Denise, a presenter for BBC Sport, Ian, an interior decorator who had been brilliant at helping me with the house, and Colin, a dog-groomer. But I tended only to meet up with them during the day and it was the evenings I hated, when George went to bed early and I was left rattling around the house on my own. I'd watch my soaps or beaver away in the kitchen making cakes for George. My 70-year-old neighbour would often come round to keep me company – he'd have a hot toddy and I'd have a glass of wine. He was very sweet, but I did long for the laughs and gossip I shared with my girlfriends.

I often felt very lonely. This was worse at the weekends, when George would fly back to London for his Sky work and I was basically trapped at the house because I had Red to look after. Sometimes my mum would come over and keep me company. Sometimes I'd go to an auction with George's sister Barbara and pick up a few more things for the house. George would usually have taken a look round first and suggested what he would like. One time he had set his heart on a butter churn. I had to wait ages for the lot to come up and then some other man started bidding against me! I was victorious, but probably paid way over the odds for it. Sometimes I would be able to leave Red with Colin and fly back with George; those were the best times.

I tried to keep busy and block out the negative feelings – George loved it here, and that's what mattered, wasn't it? I got involved with an Aids charity that Colin had been responsible for setting up. Aids 2000 raises money for counselling services for people who are HIV positive and for respite days for families and partners. It seems that in Northern Ireland there is still a stigma attached to the condition and a lot of ignorance surrounding it, meaning that people with HIV find it hard to get help and support. I took part in various fund-raising activities, including a very scary but exhilarating sky dive from thirteen thousand feet! George was enormously proud of me for doing it and kept boasting about me to everyone. Eventually, Colin asked me to be patron of the charity – I agreed, and now every year on World Aids Day we have a red ribbon ball or another big event to raise money. George is held in such high regard in Northern Ireland that the fact that I was his wife and was involved with the charity helped to boost its profile considerably.

To occupy myself for the rest of the time, I hired a personal trainer and went running every morning on the beach, with Red. I became very fit but it was a bit of an endurance test going out in the freezing cold wind. Sometimes I would literally feel as if it was going to blow me away and I would be clinging to the side of the house. I threw myself once more into my cooking. Carol, George's sister, lived down the road and through going round to her house for tea I was inspired to cook some of the Irish specialities that George loved, such as soda and potato breads, wheaten bread, pies and cakes. Now, instead of having supper at eight, George and I had tea at six. Just as well I did run every day as I needed to burn off those extra calories from all that comfort food!

Even cooking wasn't easy here, though. It was a three-hour round trip to my nearest supermarket, so I had to plan my meals for the whole week and just do a weekly shop. But it drove me mad when I wanted to cook a particular meal and discovered that I had forgotten a crucial ingredient. I'd be halfway through preparing a Thai feast and find that I hadn't got any coconut milk, so I'd have to make an SOS call to Carol to pick me some up on her way home from work – I was hardly likely to find any at the garage down the road! It sounds like such a small thing, but it made me feel even more homesick for Chelsea, where I had everything on my doorstep. Also, I had to make the supermarket trips on my own. Going shopping with George was hopeless – he was like the pied piper, and by the time we'd get to the checkout we'd have fifty people following us, all desperate to talk to their hero and get an autograph. That wouldn't have been so bad, but Irish supermarkets have certain tills that are designated for alcohol, and, if I was buying a few bottles of wine because we had guests or because I fancied the odd glass in the evening, I'd feel incredibly self-conscious, aware of everyone watching me, thinking that I shouldn't be buying wine with a husband like George Best.

Maybe I would have found life easier in Northern Ireland if George had been physically fit – at least I wouldn't have felt so lonely in the evenings. In February 2001, however, things took a turn for the worse when George contracted pneumonia. For the first time since our move he had decided to come with me when I took Red out for his morning walk. Typically, it poured with rain and George got soaked through. By the following day he felt terrible: he couldn't stop coughing, was gasping for breath and he could hardly move. I called the doctor out straight away, knowing that with George's weakened immune system we couldn't take any chances. Within hours he was admitted to Belfast City Hospital and diagnosed with severe pneumonia. I think both our hearts sank when we realised that he would have to stay in for a couple of weeks. By then we'd had enough of hospitals. George seemed very low at that time; he must have felt as if he was never going to get better. As usual, he wanted me with him all day, which was very hard, as I had no one to look after Red and the hospital was an hour and a half away. In the end Phil came over to help me out. Between us we managed to keep George entertained and well fed with delicious lunches from his favourite restaurant, but he was depressed all the same.

When he came out of hospital, to my absolute horror he started drinking again, even though he was physically very weak. I had prayed that this would never happen again, but looking back it was inevitable that it did and I think I was waiting for it. I'd already had my suspicions earlier in the year when my parents had come over and I had cooked dinner. George was away so I decided to make coq au vin – usually I couldn't use any alcohol in anything I was preparing for George. He was on tablets that were supposed to suppress his craving for alcohol, but they obviously weren't working because as I pulled a bottle of wine from the wine rack I discovered that it was empty and that the seal had been replaced. With growing anxiety I examined all the bottles in the rack and all six of them were empty.

What, you may ask, was I doing with wine in the house at all? Well, George was adamant that he wanted me to be able to enjoy the odd glass of wine – in fact, it was he who stocked the wine rack. He even had a bar built in his snooker room, although it didn't have any alcohol in it. He seemed to want to surround himself with images of drink – so many of the pictures he bought for the house were of pub scenes; he even got hold of a Guinness clock. He knew that drink was killing him, but he just couldn't seem to exorcise it from his life.

He'd barely been out of hospital a week when he took off to London. I heard from a friend that he was drinking at The Phene Arms and then he turned up drunk at my parents', telling them what a horrible person I was. 'She's certainly not that,' my mum retorted angrily, but later told me that he was very convincing and had she not known me so well she might have believed him. I was devastated. I'd had nearly a year of happiness with this new man, a year of a new marriage, and now he seemed to be intent on destroying everything. When he finally came back he apologised, but carried on going to the local pub for a couple more days. Then he stopped. But I feared the worst. I was right to as well, because two weeks later he went on a massive bender.

Looking back, all the events seem to blur into one, like some dreadful recurring nightmare. There was nothing I could do to stop him; nothing I said got through to him; I tried marching into the pub to haul him out, I begged him to come home, but he wouldn't move. Barbara and her husband Norman tried reasoning with him. Even Carol, who hadn't ever set foot in a pub in her life because she was so staunchly religious, went to the local to try and get him to see sense. But he was blind to everything except his need to drink. All I could do was stay at home, wait for him to come back and worry. I was in torment over the damage he was doing to himself, terribly afraid that he would drink and drive, and I was angry and upset. I had given up everything for this move – my family and friends – and it felt like he was throwing it back in my face. I started discovering bottles of wine around the house that he had stashed away in cupboards in rooms I never went to, and even in the pile of logs outside. Our beautiful house was a sham; it didn't mean anything if he was going to drink like this again.

'What the hell's going on?' I shouted as I walked into the living room, after returning from walking Red. It was full of about ten men I had never seen before in my life, sitting around on my sofas, smoking away and surrounded by crates of beer. I rushed upstairs. George was passed out on the bed. How dare he violate my house like this? I ran downstairs and told them in no uncertain words to get out.

When George finally came round we had a furious row. He immediately became very aggressive and punched me so hard that I fell to the floor. As I lay there shaking, Red lay on top of me, trying to protect me. George staggered out of the house, leaving me in tears. I couldn't believe we were back to having these arguments again. Half an hour later, when I'd finally pulled myself together, one of the neighbours called round in a complete state. Apparently, George had been walking in the middle of the road and the neighbour had nearly run him over. He had tried to bring him home, but George had insisted on going to the pub.

I couldn't stay at the house any longer. It felt like a prison. I had nowhere to escape to, no friends to call up, no family close by. I felt totally betrayed; I had invested so much in our marriage and he seemed hellbent on destroying it. I hated him then for his selfishness. When he was locked into this cycle of drinking I didn't mean anything to him – he just saw me as the evil ogre who wouldn't let him drink.

Well, I'd had enough. If you want to drink, I thought to myself, get on with it, I'm not going to stop you. I phoned Barbara and told her that I had to go back to London, that being around George was stressing me out so much I thought I'd have a nervous breakdown.

'I know you think I'm running away,' I told her, 'but it's the only way to bring him to his senses. If I'm not around, eventually he'll wonder where I am.' It had worked in the past. But I really didn't know if it would again.

I had a wretched time back at my parents'. I was desperately worried about George. I kept expecting him to call me, but I didn't hear anything. Then I had a phone call. It was Phil, and he sounded frantic. 'Alex, I've just heard the most terrible news from a journalist. They told me George is dead.'

I felt my legs give way and I felt sick to my stomach. Oh my God, please don't let this be true, please. I immediately called Carol. Thank God, she told me he was OK. But I knew then that I had to be with him. Hard as it was watching him drink himself senseless, I couldn't leave him to it.

When I arrived back in Ireland I was confronted with a shocking scene. George was lying in bed surrounded by dozens of empty wine bottles. He looked awful; his face was even more yellow, his feet were swollen and he stank of booze. 'What are you doing to yourself, George?' I cried. He was so out of it he couldn't answer. I made him some food and tried to get him to eat something. Then I cleared away all the empty bottles, trying to bring a semblance of normality to our bedroom and to the rest of the house.

I was interrupted by a knock on the door. I opened it to discover one of the priests. I really wasn't in the mood for a sermon. 'I'd just like a friendly personal chat,' he began. I was about to say it wasn't a good time, but he quickly got the point. 'I would like you to consider burying George in our churchyard. I'm going to keep a plot free for him.'

My mouth fell open in amazement. 'He's not dead yet, you know!' I replied.

I can only imagine he was thinking of all the visitors George's grave would attract – all those potential souls to save, and all those donations to the church. It was very enterprising of him, but hardly what I wanted to hear. I said I really couldn't think about anything like that at the moment and I shut the door. I was sure George would see the funny side of it when he was better, but, as I looked at him passed out in bed, that seemed like an impossible dream. It took him a couple more days to sober up and then I arranged for us to see Professor Williams, whom I'd been speaking to regularly throughout this latest binge.

'What happened, George?' Professor Williams asked when we went to see him at the beginning of April. There was no judgement or criticism in his voice, just concern. George simply replied that he'd felt depressed, that he'd craved a drink and that added to the depression because he knew he shouldn't. I think we all realised that George needed drastic measures to stop him drinking and so Professor Williams suggested that he try Antabuse implants. These are very powerful tablets that are sewn into a patient's stomach and are a last resort to stop them drinking – if they do drink, they are violently sick and even risk dying. I was praying that George would agree; I really didn't see how else he could beat his addiction. To my delight, he did. I threw my arms around him and said, 'Thank you!'

He had to see a psychiatrist in order to check that he was mentally stable, because the implants are potentially so dangerous. He was given a clean bill of mental health, although some antidepressants were prescribed to help his depression. The Professor really wanted George to check into The Priory for an extensive course of counselling, but I knew that it would be impossible to get him there, never mind keep him there. George had never shown any desire to go down the counselling route – while it works for so many people, he had decided it was never going to work for him.

Because of his spectacular fall off the wagon, the press once again went wild and were clamouring at our door for interviews. I found that the easiest way of coping with them was to present our story as simply and honestly as I could, and so I recorded an interview with Trevor MacDonald about George's latest binge, hoping to draw a line under the whole affair.

George had the operation to have the implants a few weeks later, and the tablets were sewn into his stomach. He would have to have them replaced every three months. They are so powerful that we were warned not to let George come into any contact with alcohol; it couldn't be in his food, or even in his aftershave or deodorant. For a few weeks back in Ireland George had to stay in bed – initially, the pellets caused him a lot of pain and he felt weak anyway after his binge. I was back to being his nurse.

Gradually he started to get stronger and feel better. He asked me to get him a painting set to keep him occupied and for a while he painted every day – his pictures were surprisingly good – but then he lost interest.

Our relationship seemed to be back on track, his recent binge a distant memory. I felt more relaxed now he'd had the implants, because I knew he couldn't drink – and if he did I would know about it instantly. All in all, he seemed to be in a better mood because he knew that a drink was out of the question.

One of the highlights of that year was definitely our wedding anniversary in July. George told me he had booked a surprise and that I had to pack smart clothes and beach things. He was so excited and I couldn't wait to find out where we were going. But the morning we were due to set off from the Gatwick Hilton he was terribly ill. He was sick and his feet and legs swelled up from the water retention; in fact, he could barely put his shoes on. He insisted on going off on his own to change some money for our trip. I told him I would go instead, but he didn't want me to find out where we were going. I took one look at his face when he finally staggered back into our hotel room and I said we couldn't possibly go anywhere. But George made light of how he felt and told me we had to go to the train station. I felt a slight pang of disappointment; I thought we would be jetting off somewhere exotic. How guilty did I feel when he revealed that we were going on the Orient Express to Venice!

We had the most romantic, magical time together. I was thrilled to be travelling on that famous train – it had long been a dream of mine, and it lived up to all my expectations. We had our own luxurious carriage and butler to wait on us, and the food was exquisite – we both feasted on caviar, which we loved. In the evenings we'd sit in the piano bar talking and holding hands and the next day we'd be woken up with breakfast in bed. It was so exciting opening the blind, not knowing what country you were going to be travelling through.

We arrived in Venice and I discovered that George had booked us into a stunning hotel by the lido. He was well aware of my addiction to sunbathing, and this was the one part of Venice that actually had a beach. By this time, though, George could barely walk, his feet and legs were getting even more swollen. He would sit next to me under an umbrella on the beach for a few hours and then would have to retire to bed. But apart from George feeling poorly we had an idyllic time; everything had been perfect and we'd got our fix of sunshine as well.

By now we were resigned to the fact that there wasn't going to be a summer in Ireland – even in July it was so cold there that I had to have a log fire going. Finally, however, the sun shone and we rushed out and bought garden furniture and sun loungers and were busy planning our first barbecue. I happened to remark to our neighbour, 'How nice, summer has finally arrived.'

He replied, 'What do you mean? Today is the summer!'

And he was right, it was – we never had another day like it. It really got us down. I've always loved the sun and George has too; he was just as much of sun-worshipper as me and because he was so poorly he really felt the cold.

The house was perfect, I liked the country and I had made some good friends, but I'd had enough of being stuck in the middle of nowhere and I'd definitely had enough of the weather. My friend Ian showed me a gorgeous house that was for sale near where he lived, where the weather was much more temperate. But as George and I drove to see it he said, 'Shall we move back home?'

I felt a huge weight lifted from my shoulders. 'I'm so pleased you've said that! Yes please.'

I didn't regret the year we had spent in Ireland. I believe that it had definitely helped George battle his addiction and working on the house together had brought us closer than we had ever been before. But I was delighted to be moving back to England. We decided to start house-hunting in Surrey, close to my parents. This time I hoped we would find a house where we could start our family. By November we had found it – a beautiful converted barn, tucked away on a private road and surrounded by fields but within half an hour of London. We could enjoy the best of both worlds. We put an offer in, which was accepted, and I started to get excited about our return.

George's health continued to deteriorate, though. It was becoming clear that the doctors' hopes that his liver might rejuvenate were not going to be fulfilled. In November we went to Cyprus, where George had a business engagement. It should have been a pleasant break for us, a chance to catch some winter sun and relax. But within a day George became violently ill with agonising stomach pains and a raging temperature. I was so alarmed by the state of him that I called a doctor, who told me to get him immediately to hospital. Once there he was admitted straight into intensive care. 'Here we go again!' I groaned to myself. I hated seeing George suffering like this. The only good thing was that the doctor in Cyprus knew Professor Williams very well and so was able to talk to him about George's condition, which reassured us all.

They kept him in for a week – he had some kind of gastric bug, made worse by his weakened immune system. Wryly, I thought that I could write a book on leading hospitals of the world after the amount of time I had spent in them in the past year.

Back home, Professor Williams had some serious news for us. George wasn't going to get better; he was only going to get worse. A liver transplant was the only thing that could save him now. As soon as he said George was going to be put on the waiting list, alarm bells went off in my head. I had this horrible feeling that as soon as he recovered from the operation he would drink again. The Professor looked intently at George and said, 'But, if you drink again, I'm going to have to move to New Zealand!' He was obviously joking, convinced that no one would throw away a second chance like that...

CHAPTER THIRTEEN

A SECOND CHANCE

I tried to put worries about George drinking again out of my mind. I was more concerned about him getting the transplant in the first place; many people die while they're still on the waiting list. I was really scared of him dying, but we didn't talk about it – I think it was too painful for us to openly acknowledge, but in one of his columns for the *Mail on Sunday*, George let his feelings out:

> *The most important things in the world to me are my wife, my son, my family and my friends. I know that sounds corny but I mean it from the heart. This last year has been a second chance for me, a second chance for life. It started the day I went into the clinic and told Professor Williams I wanted Antabuse implants permanently.*
>
> *At that point Alex knew our lives were going to*

be different. That the behaviour of the past was in the past. I've never told Alex this but she has saved my life. She saw the good in me when others wouldn't. And she's stayed with me when most others couldn't. Even if I feel terrible every day, I say a big thank you to God. I have been so lucky to find her. I've never regretted a day I've been with her.

He went to talk about how he longed to have children with me and how he'd be a better father second time around. Then he talked directly about dying:

I'd hate leaving Alex behind. This is the first time I've been truly in love. I felt it straight away with her. It was a hell of a decision to be together. There was my track record, the age difference, my drinking. Everything was against us. But seven years on we're still together. And things have got better and better.

I wept as I read his words. It was all true; he was the great love of my life and we had been through so much together. All I wanted was for him to have the operation and recover so that we could have the second chance I thought we deserved. A second chance to have the children we both wanted. As I was fast approaching thirty, I was conscious of my biological clock ticking away and I was desperate for us to start a family. I hoped that when he was well that might be possible. It certainly wasn't at the moment. Sex, which had played such a major part in our relationship, had almost fizzled out completely. George was simply too ill and exhausted, and to be honest, when you're looking after someone as I had been looking after George, you stop thinking of them as a sexual being. Our love for each other had changed and matured – we'd become more of a partnership. We were incredibly close because we spent all our time together, so much so that we often thought the same things or said the same things. I didn't worry about the sex; I was sure that when he was better it would resume.

I knew there were some people who didn't believe George should be on the transplant list because his illness was self-inflicted. But it's not as simple as that – alcoholism is a disease and George had tried everything to beat it. Doesn't everybody deserve a second chance? Just because George was famous and everyone knew about his alcoholism, why shouldn't he have one too? A very high percentage of liver transplants are performed on alcoholics; he wasn't the first one to need this life-saving treatment and he was on the waiting list like everybody else.

During those long months of waiting for his operation I was kept going by the dream that he would recover, that he wouldn't drink and that we would have the children we longed for. Looking back now, I feel intense sadness that it remained exactly that – a dream.

For the next eight months we were in limbo. We were given a pager so the hospital could beep us if a suitable organ became available, and we had to give them all our contact details. We weren't allowed to go abroad and if we went away in this country we had to notify the hospital. We had to be able to get to the hospital as quickly as possible if the call came. It was quite overwhelming knowing that we were waiting for someone to die so that George could be given a second chance of life.

We moved into Flint Barn the day after my 30th birthday, in January 2002. I'd celebrated this milestone in quite a low-key way, by having a meal out with close friends and family; to be honest, I didn't want to acknowledge my age! George felt so poorly that he had to leave early and go home to bed. I think he was starting to feel guilty that his being ill was holding me back and stopping me from enjoying myself. He would frequently tell me to go out, but I really didn't want to leave him on his own and he was much too unwell to come out and socialise with me. He spent most of the time in bed or lying on the sofa in front of the fire, and I stayed with him. But it was no sacrifice – I wanted to be with him; besides, my family and friends would often pop by to keep me company.

He decided that he wanted another puppy, and so we bought Rua, another red setter. I already walked one dog, I reasoned, one more wouldn't make much difference. It was worth it, seeing how much George loved the dogs. They were so pampered and spoiled and even had their own bed in our bedroom!

George's illness aside, we felt happy and settled in our

new house. Unlike our Irish home, we didn't have to do anything to it and the style and layout suited us perfectly. I had a beautiful large kitchen as my kingdom, and George had a little snug where he could retire with the dogs and watch the football and his favourite quiz shows. There was a spacious living room with a lovely fireplace; two good-sized bedrooms, several bathrooms and an extensive garden. I liked it all the more for being a converted barn, with its high ceilings and beams. It wasn't a conventional family house, but nor were we a conventional couple.

In the past, one of the ways George had dealt with not drinking was to plan lots of trips away. Now he had the Antabuse to stop him, but even though he felt so ill he was still restless staying in the same place. By April we were both going a little stir-crazy and when George was offered the chance to do a speech at the Dubai World Cup races we were eager to go. Professor Williams only gave us permission after the organisers promised to fly us back in their private jet if the call came. It was just the break we needed, and we had an excellent time with Paul and Stacy Young, Mike Rutherford from Genesis and his wife Angie and Kenny Jones from The Who. And, even though George felt poorly, he still managed to hold on to his sense of humour. When I asked him if he wanted to look at the duty free, he replied, 'It's no use to me: I can't drink, chocolates might have alcohol in them, I can't wear aftershave, and I don't smoke!' Point taken.

We definitely needed things we could look forward

to, to take our minds off the endless waiting and the fact that George was getting sicker, so in May we decided to throw a house-warming party. The guest list spiralled out of control and, just as I was wondering how I was going to cater for everyone, George decided we would put up a marquee and hire caterers and a team of chefs. 'Alex,' he said, 'you always do everything, this time you relax, let someone else do the work – enjoy the party.'

I certainly did! Barbara Windsor, Jimmy Tarbuck, Gail Porter and Susan George were among the guests and George's family came over from Ireland. It was a great day. George made a huge effort to appear well and for once I could put my worries about the transplant out of my mind. In the morning, for the first time ever, George made me breakfast in bed – egg with soldiers. It was a rare treat being looked after.

Of course, our party was on a slightly smaller and less lavish scale than the one we were invited to later that month – the Beckhams' World Cup party! It had a Japanese theme and guests had to wear white tie or diamonds. I wore a gorgeous black strapless dress by Roland Mouret and bought a fabulous pair of princess shoes, silver with diamonds suspended from the straps – paste, I'm afraid. I also wore a rather lovely diamond necklace, but again it was costume jewellery, though I'd like to think that you couldn't tell the difference! It was a night devoted to star-spotting, an A–Z of celebs. You name them, they were there. Elton John came up to me and said, 'Hi, gorgeous',which made my night. George was chuffed because David Beckham is such a huge fan of his. All in all it was a very good party, except for one thing – neither George nor I like sushi, and that's what was served. So, when we left after dinner because George was feeling exhausted, we had to get fish and chips because we were both famished. I was a little miffed a few days later when one of the papers printed a photograph of me at the party and pointed out that Victoria wasn't drinking because she was pregnant, David wasn't drinking because he had a match, George wasn't drinking – of course – but there I was sipping a glass of champagne! I only had a couple of glasses; it hardly made me the antichrist!

By mid-July, and nearly seven months on the waiting list, we felt like the transplant was never going to happen. I hated seeing him deteriorate before my eyes – my once robust, healthy husband could now barely walk to the end of the garden without becoming exhausted. He was aching and feeling sick most days and having more off-days than good ones. We both decided that we wanted to do something special to celebrate our wedding anniversary. I suppose there was an unspoken feeling between us that this might be our last. The weather had been getting us down and we longed for blue skies and sunshine to lift our spirits. We asked Professor Williams for permission to go to Malta, somewhere we had spent many happy times. He agreed when we said we could get home in a matter of hours if need be. It was bliss to have a change of scenery, as, much as I loved our new house, I was getting sick of being there constantly.

I woke on the morning of our anniversary to a knock on the door from room service. I opened it and discovered a waiter pushing a trolley with breakfast, a bottle of champagne and an enormous bunch of flowers. He then proceeded to set out breakfast on our balcony, pouring a single glass of champagne for me.

'Happy anniversary, Alex,' George said, taking me in his arms.

'Happy anniversary, Bestie,' I replied, kissing him.

The surprises didn't end there, though. When we sat down to breakfast George handed me a little leather jewellery box. I opened it to discover a beautiful pair of ruby and diamond earrings. He was such a romantic – and with such great taste! I had also bought him a present – a special glass for him to drink the milkshakes he had become addicted to. Well, I like to think that it's the thought that counts!

We were supposed to be staying for seven days, but two days before we were due to depart we both decided we wanted to cut our stay short. It was very fortunate that we did, because two days after we flew back we got the phone call from the hospital we had been waiting for. They had a donor liver.

We had arrived back from Malta to a gloriously hot weekend. I'd thrown a barbecue for our friends so they could see our new pond and sample our new spa. Everyone was having such a good time, but I couldn't shake off a feeling of apprehension. Whenever there was a weekend with good weather, or whenever there was a bank holiday, I would start anticipating a call – the grim fact is that there are more fatal road accidents at these times than at any other.

On Sunday night the Professor rang to let us know that they had a potential donor. He told us to stand by and that he would call once they had more information. George and I held each other tightly. I so wanted him to have the transplant and get well, but mixed with that was sadness that someone else had died. Neither of us could sleep that night. I had finally dozed off around 6am when George came and woke me; the Professor had just called him.

'This is it,' George said.

Immediately, I leaped out of bed and started getting our things together. We had been thinking about this moment for so long and I thought I was prepared, but I still found myself running around like a headless chicken, throwing things into a bag, unable to think straight about what I was doing. Stupidly, at one point I even said, 'Do you think I've got time to wash my hair?' As if that mattered at a time like this!

We dropped the dogs off at my parents' house and I drove us to London. We were silent most of the way, deliberately not talking about the operation, though George admitted he was nervous and I felt sick inside.

By 8am we were at the Cromwell Hospital and George was immediately given a series of blood tests and a heart check. Things were moving very quickly. I called Phil and he came as fast as he could. I was only able to leave a message on Calum's mobile. By ten past ten, George was being wheeled into theatre. He kissed me and I said, 'I love you.' He replied, 'I love you too,' and then we had to say goodbye. As soon as he went into theatre the floodgates opened and I gave in to the tears and emotion. I was so afraid that he wouldn't survive the operation. After all, this was major surgery and by now he was so weak.

The surgeon, Dr Heaton, came to see me. He was a lovely man, with the most gentle, reassuring manner. He said that he would keep us informed of George's progress and that the operation would take five hours. But half-past two came and went and still no one had appeared to tell us anything. By now Calum had got my message and had joined us. The time seemed to go by so slowly. None of us wanted to talk and we just paced the room, lost in our own thoughts. Please let him be OK, I prayed. The waiting was agony.

Finally, at half-past seven, Dr Akeel Alisa, the Professor's registrar, arrived to tell us that George had another hour to go. He said that he was fine now but at one point it had been touch and go and they had nearly lost him. He had suffered massive internal bleeding. Because his liver wasn't functioning properly, his blood didn't clot as it should and his high blood pressure meant he bled more quickly. He had lost an awful lot of blood and needed to have a transfusion of forty pints because he had haemorrhaged so badly.

'He is all right now, though, isn't he?' I said, almost overcome with emotion at the thought that he had nearly died. Akeel reassured me that he was and finally, at nine o'clock, we were allowed to see George.

The transplant co-ordinator had spent several hours with us in the months before the operation, preparing George and me for what would happen. In particular, she had to prepare me for what George would look like immediately after the operation. He would be in intensive care, hooked up to a ventilator and not breathing for himself, there would be a tube in his mouth and he would still be under the anaesthetic. She said I would find it very stressful seeing him like this. Even with her explanation it was incredibly upsetting seeing George lying in intensive care – he looked so fragile and helpless, hooked up to the ventilator, unconscious. My eyes filled with tears as I looked at him. Calum broke down completely, as he hadn't known what to expect.

The nurses told me I could touch his hand. I was apprehensive about passing on germs, knowing how vulnerable he was, but they assured me it was best for him to have physical contact. He was going to be kept sedated until the following morning. I didn't want to leave his side, but the medical staff insisted that I go and get some rest, because over the next few days he would really need my support and I would be no good to him if I was totally exhausted. Even though I knew they were right, I hated leaving him. I gently kissed his forehead and told him that I loved him. Phil, Calum and I left, devastated.

When I got back to my hotel room, I was shattered

but I couldn't sleep, and just as I was finally drifting off my mobile rang. My heart jumped. Oh my God, was it the hospital with bad news? This was the crucial time for George, because the new liver could so easily be rejected by his body.

Fortunately, it was just George's friends from the States checking on his progress. I lay back down in bed, desperate for a few hours' sleep, but at 6am the press rang for an update. No rest for me, then.

A few hours later I went to see him. He was still pretty out of it and still on the ventilator. The nurses wanted me to talk to him to help bring him round very gently, then they could gradually get him to start breathing on his own. Finally, George opened his eyes and squeezed my hand weakly. My husband was back. The nurses had to keep telling him to breathe, though, and he was getting frustrated because he couldn't talk with the tube in his mouth. Already he looked different. He was still quite swollen with water retention, but his skin, which had been yellow and jaundiced, was looking pink, as if it was coming back to life. You could actually see his new liver was working.

Despite being in pain, he still had his sense of humour. The nurses had switched on the radio to keep him awake and Magic FM played one of his favourite songs, Louis Armstrong's 'What a Wonderful World'. George held up his hands and did a little jig with them. It made us all smile. My brave husband.

It was agonising for George when they took the ventilator out of his throat. He was extremely thirsty, but he was only allowed to suck absorbent sticks for moisture. By the evening, though, he was fully *compos mentis*.

'Alex,' he said, 'when I was in theatre, I had such a strange dream. I was travelling through this bright white light and then suddenly something pulled me back.'

I didn't want to scare him by saying that he had nearly died during the surgery, but it was clear he'd been through some kind of out-of-body experience. Instead, I told him I'd brought the papers in to read to him. Immediately his face fell and he said he expected they were critical about him having the operation.

'On the contrary,' I replied, 'they are all positive, and are wishing you a speedy recovery.' And it's true, they all seemed to think that George deserved his second chance.

We later found out just how lucky George had been. Before he had the operation the doctors had given him just three months to live – not that they had told us – but, after the surgeon saw the alcohol-ravaged state of his liver, they said he wouldn't even have lasted that long without the transplant. It really had been life-saving surgery.

After a day in intensive care, George was moved into a regular room and once more my life started to revolve around hospital visits. Yet again he was inundated with flowers and get-well cards. Elton John and his partner David Furnish sent a beautiful orchid and a card that read: 'Remember to look after your second chance, George.' It was a sentiment shared by all of us who cared for him. I just prayed he would.

A couple of days after the operation George said that he really wanted to make up for what he'd put me through during the years of drinking and the times of illness. He said he bitterly regretted hurting me, and hated thinking back on some of the things he had said and done. We were even planning a marriage blessing to mark the start of our new life.

He was in hospital for just under three weeks, which seems quite a short time for such major surgery, and we had a lot to learn. He was on an incredible amount of medication at first – some forty pills a day and they all had to be taken at different times, some before food, some with, some after. You needed to be a pharmacist to keep track of them all! In the past I had always taken charge of his medication, but this time the doctors made it clear that he should take responsibility, as he would have to be on the tablets for the rest of his life. At the time I thought, I'll always be there to help him; now, I think it's fortunate that the doctors made him be so self-sufficient...

Then there was the list of vital dos and don'ts George was going to have to stick to. He would have to take immuno-suppressant drugs for the rest of his life to prevent his body from rejecting his new liver; visit the dentist every three months to avoid infections; ensure all his food was well cooked. The long list of restrictions included not drinking alcohol or eating shellfish, raw eggs, soft or blue cheese, because of the bacteria they can harbour; he could not sit in the sun, because the anti-rejection drugs had lowered his immune system to such a level that he would be unable to combat skin cancer. We were actually given a handbook that set out the new rules for him to live by. It was all quite mind-boggling.

Because George wasn't well enough to write his column for the *Mail on Sunday*, I had to fill in for him and he didn't like it one little bit! I actually think the thought of me writing it another week spurred him on to make more of an effort when the physiotherapist came round to help him move and get stronger. Usually he would do anything to avoid a session, even pretending to have already done a circuit when she turned up.

We had been warned about many of the side-effects from the operation and the medication, but there was one the doctors didn't tell us about. I walked into George's room one day and he wasn't his cheery self at all. Eventually, he told me what the problem was – his testicles had swollen up to the size of melons. You know how precious men are about that part of their anatomy! He was not a happy bunny – I think he was more anxious about them than he had been about the actual transplant. Fortunately, it wasn't anything serious, just a side-effect from the operation, and we were told they would eventually shrink back to normal size. In the meantime I was dispatched to Marks & Spencer to purchase some new pants. Phil came along with me, but refused to stand with me at the checkout, in case the cashier thought that the extra-extra-large pants were for him! They certainly were the biggest pair I have ever seen. And when George was back to normal in that department, we all had a good laugh about them.

He was discharged on 17 August. When he arrived home he was so weak he could barely walk from the car to the house. He looked like a frail old man. He had lost so much weight and his face looked gaunt. I put him straight to bed. In the night he woke up moaning in agony, complaining of unbearable stomach pains. I was terrified that his body was rejecting the liver, so I phoned Professor Williams in a compete panic. He also sounded concerned and told me to bring him straight in if he got any worse. By the early morning George had deteriorated further – now, along with the stomach ache, he had a raging temperature. I took him straight back to hospital.

The doctors discovered that his bile duct had become disconnected from his liver, so all the toxic bile was going straight into his stomach. This is a life-threatening condition and, if we hadn't gone to hospital when we did, he would have died.

George said he was in more agony than he had been after his liver transplant. They had to put in a tube to drain the bile that had built up because there was so much of it. He needed to have an endoscopy to put in a stent (an expandable wire-mesh tube) to reconnect the tube. This is performed by passing a tube down your throat when you are conscious, so you can imagine how painful it is. Unfortunately, the first one didn't take, so he had to have another one. George was then kept in hospital for another two weeks. By now, I think we were both starting to feel that he was never going to get better.

Finally, he was allowed home. He still needed to have the bile drained from his body, though, so nurse Alex Best was issued with a plastic gloves and measuring jug to collect and measure the bile and keep the hospital updated on how much there was. I used to be squeamish; I'm not any more! George called me Nurse Bestie and I was – I looked after his every need, cooked his meals to fit round the times he needed to take his medication and dispensed his drugs. And, exhausting as it could be, I did it all willingly. We used to joke that we were playing doctors and nurses, because by then George had been awarded a doctorate from Queen's University in Belfast.

George not only had the physical effects of the surgery to cope with, but the doctors also stressed that there were bound to be psychological implications as well. We were both given some counselling to help with these and to help George cope with possible post-operative depression, which apparently could give him feelings of guilt. We were advised to speak to someone who had already had a transplant, but George felt too embarrassed to talk to a stranger about such things, and so we didn't.

I felt such gratitude towards the donor's family for making the decision to donate their organs – they were so brave. We had the option of writing to the family to thank them, but, again, George didn't want to. Given what happened a year after the transplant, thank God he didn't. I think it would have destroyed them knowing that their loved one's organ had gone to someone intent on a course of self-destruction...

For the rest of 2002 George was very weak and pretty much confined to the house. It was my mission to build him up. He'd lost so much weight that he really was a shadow of his former self. I threw myself into cooking delicious healthy meals for him and I baked endless cakes, to which George rapidly became addicted and he'd end up having several large slices every day! His milkshake addiction continued and I would have to make endless varieties of these. Very gradually he started to look a little better.

Towards December he was getting stronger and he was able to help me prepare for our first Christmas in the barn. I decided that we would have my family over and I wanted the occasion to be as special as possible. We weren't only celebrating Christmas, but George's recovery too. We went out to Harrods and bought lots of decorations for the house and the tree, and by the time we'd finished the house looked wonderfully festive.

That year I'd had my eye on a rather gorgeous ring, and I hinted heavily to George that I would love a new engagement ring. He shrugged and said he wasn't going to get me a ring, but privately he asked my mum to point out which one I had liked. Come Christmas Day I eagerly ripped open all my presents from him, but there was no ring. He left it until seven o'clock in the evening to hand it to me. Well, I thought, the best things are always worth waiting for. It was the perfect end to a perfect day. I'd cooked a traditional meal for the whole family and we'd all had a lovely time. I even allowed myself to think that perhaps, by the next Christmas, there would be an addition to the family. It gave me a rush of happiness to think that maybe in 2003 we would be able to have a baby.

If George found it a problem being surrounded by people drinking, he never mentioned it. Indeed, he'd get more wound up if people didn't have a drink when they were with him. Whenever we went out for dinner with family or friends, he would insist on ordering wine for us, and wouldn't let us have soft drinks. In one of his autobiographies he says he would find it much worse if people around him just drank soft drinks just because he had to. I spent the whole Christmas entertaining family and friends, culminating in having a party on New Year's Eve. It was tiring, but worth it. I've always loved entertaining.

I went to bed on New Year's Eve full of optimism about the year ahead. I was convinced it was going to be fantastic. George had a new lease of life and so did our marriage. I couldn't have imagined for a moment that in twelve months' time I would be single, my marriage in ruins and that I would have been through the worst year of my life.

CHAPTER FOURTEEN

THE WORST OF TIMES

January lived up to my expectations that this was going to be a fresh start for George and me. We were getting on better than ever and George's health was improving daily. There was so much to look forward to. At the beginning of the month, George's surgeon, Mr Heaton, asked if we would go to Switzerland to meet a group of children who had all had liver transplants. Their winter holiday was organised by a charity run by a woman called Liz, one of his former patients, who'd had a transplant some years earlier. She'd been so grateful for her second chance that she wanted to do something for children who'd also had transplants.

George and I were both moved when we met the children, some of who were very ill indeed. He definitely seemed to appreciate the chance he'd been given. However poorly the children were, they all threw themselves into the various activities; we went on a wonderful sledge ride, pulled by teams of huskies. I went skiing with some of the children and even took part in a paraglide, for which I had to go some thirteen thousand feet up a mountain and then ski down with a parachute. You go so fast you take off and it's incredibly exhilarating! One little boy who was very ill did it with me, and I so admired him for his bravery.

There was just one moment when my heart sank. We were having dinner with everybody and George saw a woman who'd had a transplant drinking a glass of red wine. He had such a look of longing on his face.

'How come she's drinking, Alex?' he asked me.

'I'm sure she shouldn't be, maybe that's why she's had to have two transplants,' I said briskly. 'You know the Professor has told you that there is no way that you can.'

It was true, George had been told this, but this was more because he was an alcoholic rather than as a consequence of the transplant. People who'd had transplants for reasons other than alcohol abuse would probably be able to drink in moderation. But there was no such thing as drinking in moderation for George. He'd even had Antabuse implants again after the transplant.

Back home, I had a big secret to keep from George. He was going to be featured on *This is Your Life*. I had a leading role in deciding who should appear and I felt like I was running a covert military operation, organising who should phone me when – all without

George finding out what was going on. In the middle of this we flew to Gran Canaria for a holiday. In the past George had liked nothing more than lying in the sun for hours at a time. But, since the transplant, those days were gone. So while I sunbathed George devoted himself to getting fit, spending hours in the gym, building up his wasted muscles. We had a romantic time together, though, and it was lovely not having to nurse him for a change.

As a way of getting him to the *This Is Your Life* studio, I had told George that he was taking part in a televised appeal for a liver charity with Professor Williams. On the big day I told him that I had a photoshoot and wouldn't be able to come with him but that I'd catch up with him later. He was totally stunned when he walked into the studio and discovered what was really going on. He had appeared on the programme in the 1960s and had always boasted that they would never catch him again. Well, they did, and he loved every minute. His whole family turned up, along with old friends including Bill Wyman, Denis Law and Bobby Macalinden, his best friend from the States. We'd even managed to get the guy who went with him to Manchester United from Northern Ireland, when the two of them were just fifteen-year-olds.

It seemed like the perfect start to the year – George was getting better, people were being very positive about him and our marriage had never been stronger. But, as his health improved, so he became restless and dissatisfied. He had begun going to the gym on a daily basis, becoming quite obsessive about it, and spending several hours there. Initially I went along with him but then I had to walk the dogs in the morning and wanted to go in the afternoon. I asked George to come with me then, but he was determined to stick to his routine of going every morning. At first he would come back after a gym session, but suddenly he started going on to the betting shop. What began as a stay of a couple of hours rapidly turned into him remaining there all day until six o'clock. It wasn't so much the money I minded about – I knew he never spent that much – it was the time. This was supposed to be our quality time, a chance to do some of the things that his long illness had prevented us doing.

One of the things that had kept me sane during those long months when I had looked after him was imagining what we could do when he was well again. And what about all those promises he had made about making up for all the bad times? I began to feel increasingly fed up. Cheers, mate, I thought to myself, I looked after you all that time and now you leave me on my own all day. It was as if we'd gone back to the bad old days of The Phene Arms, except without the alcohol. I tried talking to him about it, but he was incredibly stubborn and I knew if I pushed it he'd end up going for longer. Who knows why he did it – maybe the buzz of gambling helped deaden his craving for alcohol.

By May he was well and truly locked into his pattern of going to the betting shop every day. I was more free to do my own things now that I wasn't so worried about his health, but I wasn't happy about the situation. George seemed unable to settle at home – he wanted to be out all the time and he became obsessed with wanting to go away. He became moody and grumpy and then inevitably an argument would break out between us, even though I had no desire to quarrel. He was obviously struggling to accept the fact that he couldn't drink again, but now he was better the craving was stronger and it seemed as if he didn't know what else to do with himself. Not even our dream of having a family seemed able to distract him.

He had a big distraction, though, later that month, when the *Daily Mail* asked to do a piece about George's rapid recovery and offered to fly us anywhere we wanted to do the interview. I've always fancied Mustique, the tiny private Caribbean island and hideaway of many of the rich and famous. Mick Jagger and Tommy Hilfiger are among the A-listers with a house there and it was, of course, a favourite haunt of Princess Margaret. To my delight the paper agreed, and we found ourselves booked in for a week's stay at The Cotton House, the only hotel on the island. This has to be one of the most luxurious and exclusive hotels in the world. It's a beautiful white, colonial-style building surrounded by stunning white-sand beaches and the turquoise sea. Our suite was beautiful, with a spacious bedroom, lounge and bathroom, and we had our own balcony that looked out over the beach.

In the mornings George would work out in the gym

and I'd indulge myself sunbathing, then we'd hop on a golf buggy – the only form of transport on the island – and head off to one of the many perfect beaches. There the hotel would deliver a picnic to us and we'd eat the most delicious lunch on a totally deserted beach. In the afternoons I'd get down to some more serious tanning and catch up with some reading and George would rest in a shady hammock. In the evening we'd have dinner in the hotel's gastronomic restaurant. It was sheer self-indulgence.

Looking at George I could hardly believe what excellent progress he had made, and his body was back to being toned – especially his legs and arms. He might not have had his six pack back, but he wasn't that far off it. I felt a resurgence of desire for him and for the first time in ages we made love.

Mustique couldn't have been more perfect and I'd like to say that we had a perfect time together, but deep down I wasn't happy with the way my marriage was going. George seemed happy and carefree, but I couldn't help comparing the way he was now with the rather moody and distant man he had become at home. I longed for the intimacy we had shared during his illness – now he seemed to want to keep me at a bit of a distance. Back home, George continued to seem restless and unsettled. He just didn't seem to know how to occupy himself, even though he had plenty of offers of work now he was sober.

In June we headed off to Corfu with our family and friends. George had recently sold his European Player of the Year medal for £150,000, and we decided we wanted to buy a holiday house there. We looked at a few, one of which seemed perfect, but George didn't seem able to get into the holiday spirit or to want to spend time with us. Whenever the rest of us were relaxing and chatting by the pool, George would wander off, saying he was going for a coffee at the taverna. One day when he returned from one of his trips I was convinced I could smell alcohol on his breath.

'Give me a kiss,' I demanded from my sun lounger. He bent down to give me a reluctant peck on the cheek and I wrinkled my nose. I could definitely detect alcohol – but surely he couldn't be drinking again? The Antabuse would have made him really sick. I also noticed that he'd started chewing gum, something he had never done before.

Then Julie spotted something. We had all gone out for dinner and as usual George ordered white wine for Julie and me. As I turned round to talk to someone George picked up my glass and drained it and Julie saw him do it. He simply stared back at her as if nothing had happened and I think she almost doubted her own eyes.

She found me later. 'Alex, I don't want to worry you, but is George drinking again?' And she explained what she had seen.

In turn, I told her about smelling alcohol on his breath, but again I reassured her he couldn't have started again, because of his implants. It left me feeling very uneasy, though.

When we returned from our holiday I mentioned my

worries to Phil, but he was adamant that George couldn't possibly be drinking once more, and I felt really guilty for thinking badly of him. Then I discovered that a bottle of brandy that I was sure was full had been nearly emptied. It was deeply worrying.

And George wasn't himself. He was increasingly moody and seemed to want to pick a quarrel. I was back to feeling like I was walking on eggshells, worried that the slightest thing might provoke him. One night in July we had a row, sparked by me simply asking him what was wrong and why he was so unhappy. It got us nowhere and, sick and tired of dealing with him, I fled to Mum and Dad's. The following day I had a hair appointment in London. I was just about to walk into the salon when I thought I'd call George to check he was OK. This was the first night we had spent apart in a very long time and it really didn't feel right. George answered. He sounded paralytic, so drunk he could hardly speak, but when he realised it was me he started crying. I felt the world spin round. I tried to keep calm and I told him I'd be back as soon as I could. I raced into the salon, cancelled my appointment and drove home as fast as I could. I kept calling George to tell him that he would be all right, that I was on my way and that he should stay at the house. I was terrified that he would drive somewhere and he was in no state to be behind a wheel.

As I drove back, distraught as I was, I remember thinking quite clearly that this was probably the end of our relationship. Deep down, I knew that if he started drinking again I really couldn't stand by him as I had before. I found myself wondering who would look after him then, who would be there to pick up the pieces? Then reality kicked in and I tried to push the thought out of my head. I had to get back to him.

When I got home he was sitting in the garden with an empty bottle of wine at his feet. As soon as he saw me he tried to hide the bottle. He was in a dreadful state.

'I'm sorry, Alex,' he sobbed, 'I'm finding it so hard, not drinking, so hard.'

'I understand, darling,' I said, putting my arms around him and crying as well. I told him how much I loved him, how I understood how difficult it was for him, how I appreciated the effort he had made and how good he had been. There was nothing more I could say, so I put him to bed and made him some food.

As soon as he was safely upstairs I locked the front door and hid the keys. Then I phoned the registrar Dr Alisa. I told him George had been drinking and asked him what on earth I should do. He sounded shocked at the news, but what could he say? There was no comfort to be had. The worst thing that could happen had happened. He reminded me that George was due another lot of implants and that he was sure he would be OK after them.

As I got into bed next to George that night I had one thought in my head: Please let this be a one-off, please don't let him return to the bad old days. In the morning George promised to stop drinking, but he didn't. He carried on for the next two weeks. I thought of getting rid of all the alcohol in the house, but then I thought, If

I do that, he'll just go off God knows where. Painful as it was to watch, I would rather he drank in the house than go off in his car and end up killing somebody through drink-driving. For a while he stayed at home, sitting in his snug and working through the supplies of wine he'd obviously bought from an off-licence. Once I even saw him outside drinking Lucozade. That's a good sign, I thought, picking up the bottle, only to discover he'd filled it with brandy.

I kept imploring him to have the implants again and he promised he would, but kept finding excuses not to. In desperation I called the Professor. He knew about the situation from Akeel and was as shocked as any of us.

'Why is this happening?' I pleaded with him. 'Why isn't the Antabuse working?'

'I don't know Alex,' he replied. 'It could be that after having them for two years he has become immune to them, or we might have put them in the wrong place.'

Oh my God, I thought, if the pellets don't work any more, what hope is there that he can ever stay sober?

I was distraught by what had happened, a nervous wreck. I was dreadfully worried about George and also terrified that the press would find out. But I couldn't confine him to the house forever. Whenever I tried to hide his car keys he would fly into a rage, order a cab and go off. One night he called me as I was waiting for him in the house. He sounded drunk but wouldn't tell me where he was. I begged him to let me come and pick him up, knowing that he had his car. Eventually he told me he was at a local pub called The Chequers.

I had a horrible sense of déjà vu as I walked into the beer garden. George was sitting alone, at a table covered in glasses. I sat down.

'Please come home.'

He said he would after he'd had just one more drink. That would be his last and after that he promised to stop drinking for good. This was just a blip. But people kept coming up and offering to buy him drinks, loving the fact that George Best was at their local. And George never turned down a drink. I begged him, but he wouldn't move. 'I'll get a taxi back,' he promised. But he didn't come home that night. I lay awake all night wondering where he was, sick with worry. I kept phoning his mobile, anxious to know where he was, but he had switched it off.

He finally turned up later the next day, claiming to have spent the night in the pub. And he carried on drinking – his promise the night before had meant nothing.

The situation was tearing me apart. I told only my family and a few close friends what was going on – one of whom was Mick Hucknell. He'd been a friend of George's and later mine for years, and he had been a great fan of George. Immediately he invited me round. I think he could tell I was at my wits' end. He very sweetly cooked me dinner and told me to stay the night. The following morning, after his girlfriend had gone to work, he made me breakfast and we sat outside in the garden.

'Alex,' he said, looking serious, 'you can't be Florence Nightingale forever. It's time that you started looking after yourself.'

I nodded, thinking that maybe he was right. Knowing how close he was to George, I knew he wouldn't say such a thing lightly.

As soon as I returned home George laid into me, demanding to know where I'd been all night. When I told him, he insisted that I was having an affair with Mick. His girlfriend was there, I shouted back at him in frustration, tired of his ridiculous accusations. But he wouldn't let it drop and in the end he stormed out of the house, no doubt back to the pub. It was like history repeating itself, the pattern so predictable and painful. I thought I had endured everything that his drinking could throw at me, but things were about to get a whole lot worse.

I decided that I would have to let the *Mail on Sunday* know that George was drinking again. Up till then I had been lying for him, saying that he was too ill to write his weekly column. But I knew I couldn't cover for him forever. It was just as well I did, because the next day someone tipped off the *News of the World* that George was boozing once more, and the media feeding frenzy began.

That weekend George didn't come home at all. He spent the entire time in the pub. Ironically, I knew exactly where he was because Sky were covering the story and had a camera trained on him the whole time on their active channel, as if it were some major news event rather than someone's personal tragedy unfolding. The press also camped outside our house in their hordes. There were film crews and journalists, lights and cameras; there was even a Sky satellite dish. It was mayhem. Our house was on a private estate but was surrounded by a public bridleway, and that's where the media stayed for the next four months, charting every step of George's descent back into alcoholism and our failing marriage. It was a complete and utter nightmare – not only was I devastated by what George was doing, but also my every move was being scrutinised by the press. I felt like a prisoner in my own home. I had to resort to shutting all the curtains, but even then I could hear them all outside, talking and laughing. What did they care that my life was falling apart?

George wouldn't come home. I kept calling him, but he didn't answer his phone. Because I was the one who wanted him to stop drinking, I was the bad guy. My sister went to check up on him in the pub and told me that he was still being treated like some kind of hero, with people buying him endless drinks. They were also taking him on a tour of different pubs in the area, travelling around as if they had the FA cup in their car. He was their trophy. It was grotesque.

I called the landlord of The Chequers and asked him what the hell he thought he was doing, serving George drinks. 'You're killing him, don't you realise that?'

He was adamant that it wasn't him who served George.

It was bad enough that George was drinking again, but now he wasn't taking any of the medication to stop his body rejecting his liver either. God knows what damage he was doing to himself.

I knew that George wouldn't listen to me if I spoke to him in the pub, so Dr Alisa and Phil promised to come down and try and talk some sense into him. I was waiting anxiously for them to arrive, when Phil called to tell me that George had been arrested. Apparently, he had punched a photographer working for the *News of the World* and then smashed a camera. He was being held at Reigate police station and he wanted me to drop off his medication. I still have my uses, then, I thought bitterly.

We spent a couple of hours waiting at the police station. Finally, the *News of the World* said they wouldn't press charges against George and so he was free to go. George wouldn't travel back with us, though; he sent a message to say the police would take him home in an unmarked car so he could evade the press.

Dr Alisa and I went home. We waited and waited, but George didn't come back. I called him and discovered to my horror that the police had simply driven him back to the pub. I couldn't believe they had been so irresponsible. Dr Alisa went to try and reason with him, but it was no good – George simply said he would be home soon and then didn't move. Phil went too and was in tears imploring him to stop drinking, but he said the same thing to him. He was choosing to drink over everything else, and all the rest of us, it seemed, could go to hell. He stayed away that night as well.

On Sunday my friend Julie came over to keep me company. I told her I couldn't bear to be in the house a moment longer. We drove to a quiet restaurant, though

I couldn't eat a thing – my nerves were completely shot. As we drove back to the house the press had blocked off the road and I had to get out and push my way through them. Cameras were going off in my face and journalists were bombarding me with questions: 'Where's George, Alex?' 'How do you feel about his drinking?' It was a nightmare.

Finally, on Monday, George called me.

'Well?' I said to him, waiting to hear what he had to say, whether he had any kind of explanation for the three days of torment he had put me through.

'Do you want me to come home?'

I sighed. 'Yes, come home.'

Everyone was aghast that I could say such a thing, but the truth was if I'd had a go at him on the phone he would never have come back. He was brought home by one of his new friends from the pub, who insisted on coming into the house with George, obviously keen to have a nose around. I gave him such a filthy look that he soon left. George looked terrible and was still drunk. He decided it would be amusing to sit in the garden and look at the press camped beyond our fence. I watered the garden and tried to maintain a semblance of normality – I felt I had to do something or I would go mad. Journalists were calling out to me, asking me why I had let him back. There was even footage of us on *The Richard and Judy Show*. You really would have thought there were more important things going on in the world.

The following day, the press reported that George

had spent the weekend at some woman's house and they even had a picture of this mystery blonde.

'What's all this, George?' I demanded, thrusting the paper at him.

He insisted that there was nothing to the story, and told me she was called Gina and was the sister of one of his friends from the local and he'd gone round there with his friend because one of her children was ill. 'Alex,' he said, 'you know me. You and me will be together forever.'

The story kept niggling away at me, but I chose to believe him. I had never had any reason to think George might be unfaithful before.

He promised to stop drinking and really apologised for his behaviour. For a while, things returned to a kind of normality. He seemed to be keeping his promise, though he kept going to the betting shop every day and we still had the press camped outside and following our every move. I even had my own personal motorcyclist who would follow me wherever I went – once, I nipped to the garage to buy some milk and there he was behind me. Alex Best buys a pint of milk, hardly earth-shattering news, is it? One paper dubbed the whole saga of our marriage 'BestEnders' and in a way they were right, it was like a soap and with just as few laughs as the series they'd named us after.

George and I weren't getting on at all well. He had shattered my confidence in him by drinking again and left me feeling so hurt. I could read him like a book and I knew that now he'd had a drink after his transplant and he'd been OK – he hadn't ended up in hospital, he hadn't dropped down dead – there was nothing to stop him doing it again. He kept promising to get new implants, but then kept cancelling the appointment. No wonder he hadn't wanted to contact the donor's family. 'Thanks for the new liver, now I'm going to carry on drinking myself to death' – not exactly what they would have wanted to hear, was it?

I went to the Goodwood races for Ladies Day with a group of my girlfriends. I needed to have a break from worrying about the state of my marriage, but I didn't feel entirely relaxed. When I called to let George know I was on my way home, he told me not to rush back on his account, which was very out of character. I ignored him and came back anyway and he didn't exactly seem pleased to see me. Something was going on – I just didn't know what.

The following Sunday we were having lunch with my parents and George seemed unable to sit still. In the end he said he was going to place a bet. Then I received a message on my mobile that was obviously intended for him. It was the landlord of The Chequers, saying that they were all in The Kingswood Arms and that he should join them. Here we go again, I thought. Now my afternoon was ruined as well, so I decided to see if he was in The Kingswood Arms. He wasn't there, nor was he in The Chequers, but just as I was about to leave a taxi driver I knew called out that I'd just missed George. 'Funny business about last Thursday,' he added.

'What do you mean?' I asked. That was the day I'd

gone to Goodwood. He told me that he had taken George to Gatwick Airport, pursued by the inevitable press. He'd had to drop him off at Departures, wait for a half an hour, then pick him up at Arrivals. I tried to hide my confusion; it did indeed seem very strange behaviour.

By the time I arrived home George was back. As he was sober I didn't say anything about going to the pub and meeting the taxi driver; I didn't want to anger him and give him an excuse to drink. But something wasn't right, I knew that much.

CHAPTER FIFTEEN

BETRAYAL

The next day we flew to Malta. I hoped that if we were away we could rebuild some bridges and put the events of the past month behind us. Instead, it turned out to be a disaster, and the beginning of the end.

George continued to behave very oddly, and kept disappearing off, obviously to drink. There was no closeness between us at all. He didn't seem to want to make amends. One morning he asked me how to dial England. Instantly, I was suspicious, as George rarely picked up the phone if he could help it, so who was so important that he had to ring them? I left him lying by the pool and went to our hotel bedroom. I promptly went through his wallet and pulled out the list of important numbers I had written out for him. At the bottom of the list he'd added an unfamiliar number, but there was no name against it. Shaking, I picked up the phone and dialled, but was thrown when it was answered by a florist. I returned to the poolside and carried on brooding. I kept looking at George and wondering what was going on. Unable to relax, I returned to the bedroom. Once there, as if I knew exactly where to search, I headed straight for the drawer, where he kept his training shorts, looked in the back pocket and found a piece of paper with another number on it, one digit different from the other one I'd found. The paper was a pub receipt from The Chequers. I phoned it and this time a woman answered.

'Who's this?' I asked.

'Paula,' replied a rather rough-sounding woman.

I slammed the phone down and marched to the pool.

'Who's Paula?' I shouted at George.

'I don't know,' he said, looking shifty.

'What's this, then,' I said, waving the piece of paper in his face. He immediately accused me of snooping and I retorted that I'd every right to.

'Who is she?' I said again, feeling angrier by the second.

He replied that she was just a girl he'd met at the pub who wanted him to try and get her a job at Sky as a set designer.

Sensing there was more to it than that, I shouted back, 'Isn't that what job centres are for? Why is it up to you?'

He continued to try and talk his way out of it for the rest of the day, but I wasn't convinced; his story seemed very implausible. I couldn't get it out of my head. Even reading offered no escape – the central character in my book was called Paula!

My good friend Trudie called me that evening. 'Alex, you know we've always had that pact where we tell each other the truth about the men we're involved with?' A few years earlier I had told her that a man she was seeing had just had a baby with his girlfriend, prompting Trudie to put an abrupt end to their relationship.

I clutched my mobile tightly, dreading what she was going to come out with.

'I've just had a call from a paper warning you that there's a story about George coming out tomorrow. Apparently, he's been seeing some woman at The Chequers and they've been photographed together in the woods.'

The next few hours were like a blur. I raced down to the pool to confront George, telling him I knew exactly what he'd been up to, but he kept repeating that he didn't know what the hell I was talking about. He claimed only to have been for a walk with this woman in the woods, but as he very rarely took our dogs for a walk I couldn't believe that's all he'd been up to – walking and George really didn't go together. I didn't believe his denials and was growing more and more distraught by his betrayal. By now I was aware that we were being stalked by several journalists and photographers and I kept getting calls on my mobile from reporters desperate to get a piece of the action. I couldn't bear to stay with George and have the whole media scrum kick off around us. I went up to the hotel room and threw George's clothes out, screaming that he would have to stay somewhere else; I didn't want him near me.

'Just fly over here,' Trudie implored me when I called her again in tears. 'You can stay for as long as you need to.'

So the following morning I flew back to Gatwick, then caught a plane to Spain. The press were out in force when I landed at Gatwick. I put on my dark glasses and hid my feelings. But I wasn't going to escape that easily. I was hotly pursued by two journalists from a paper George was exclusively contracted to, and they insisted on flying to Spain with me to make sure I didn't speak to any other reporters.

'For God's sake,' I said to them, 'my marriage is falling apart, the last thing I want to do is to talk to any journalists – including you!'

But as soon as I landed in Spain I was handed a solicitor's letter from the paper reminding me that I was under contract to talk to nobody but them. We'd had some good publicity in the past, and some lovely trips, but didn't they just want their pound of flesh when it all went wrong? Some people say that if you are in the public eye you should expect to pay a price but at that moment the price seemed too high. Trudie met me at the airport and took me straight to her apartment. She tried to get me to eat something, but I couldn't.

'Have you got it?' I asked.

She knew what I meant and silently handed me a copy of the *News of the World*. George's betrayal was the front-page story: 'Best's Secret Dates with Blonde –

beauty tells of seduction,' screamed the headline. I was almost shaking too much to read it, but I forced myself; I had to know. The woman – Paula – claimed that George had been pursuing her relentlessly, chatting her up, promising her the high life of celebrity lunches and nights in hotels. He had told her that his marriage was over and he wanted to be with her. It sounded a bit too much like George for me to think that she had made it up.

It was too much. I collapsed in tears on the bed. I couldn't believe that he had done this. It was the most brutal slap in the face ever. All I had done was love him and stand by him. He was making a mockery of everything I had ever done for him and of our marriage.

I stayed with Trudie for five days. I was a wreck, unable to eat, sleep or think straight. Whenever I ventured out of the apartment I would be pursued by the press and cameras would go off in my face. 'Yes, let's get another picture of the wronged wife.' One surreal photograph that made one of the tabloids showed a picture of George reading about me in Spain as he lay by the pool. He didn't even call me to see if I was all right. He was drinking again with a vengeance and getting involved in all kinds of scrapes. One minute he'd be playing pool with the journalists, the next he would be punching them. He was spiralling out of control. I was angry and hurt, wanting explanations from George, but I knew it was pointless while he was drinking.

Then I heard that he was going home. I asked my

mum to keep on eye on him, not trusting him to look after himself or the house in his current state. She called me back, telling me I had better come back too. Apparently, the two journalists who were babysitting him to make sure he didn't talk to any other media were staying in my house! I was outraged. I flew straight back, but George obviously couldn't face seeing me and so had disappeared back to the pub, with his press minders in tow. Mum even gave him her house keys so he could stay there if necessary. She said that their house would be empty because she and Dad were going to be staying with me.

Mum and Dad did their best to comfort me when I arrived back, physically and emotionally shattered. They were determined to stay with me, but I told them I would be fine and so they went home. At two in the morning, Mum woke up. She could hear voices in the hall. She went downstairs to be confronted with a very drunken George, the so-called 'mystery blonde' – Gina, the woman he had been photographed with before we went to Malta – and her brother, with the two reporters in hot pursuit. Mum let him have it, shouting how disgusted she was by his bringing strangers into her house. They all got the message. The reporters tried to persuade George to come with them to Forest Mere, the health farm, but he had other ideas. He managed to give them the slip and went round to Gina's council house. And there he stayed for the next week, drinking all the time. As long as he had somebody to look after him who didn't mind about him drinking, then he was happy. He wanted to drink and no one, not even me, would get in the way of that. I couldn't believe that this was the same man who had told me that I was the love of his life and that we would be together forever. I was heartbroken.

Finally, George called me. I let out all the pent-up rage that had been burning inside me, screaming down the phone, 'Now there's not just one, there's two women. You lied to me all the time!' Still George insisted that he was just friends with Gina. He was now at the health farm to try and sort himself out, he said.

I didn't know what to think, or even what I should do. But even after everything he had put me through, I really missed him. I'd phone him every morning at six because I couldn't sleep and he would tell me that he was sober and that he hadn't been drinking.

Fortunately, around this time I managed to land a spot of TV presenting for *This Morning*, which gave me a good reason not to spend all day crying. To my surprise, I enjoyed the work. It gave me a buzz and took me away from the nightmare I felt I was living in.

Back home, George kept begging me to come and see him at Forest Mere. By now I wanted to. I wanted us to get back together and sort things out. I still believed that our marriage was salvageable because I loved him so much and, however much it might appear to the contrary, I knew he loved me. Also, I wanted to give it one last shot; I wasn't going to give up on him without a fight. We had been through so much over the nine years we had been together and I wasn't having any fifteen-minute wonder destroying my marriage and ruining my life.

Our meeting was intensely emotional. We held each other tight and he told me how much he loved me. It was exactly what I needed to hear. We were photographed embracing on the balcony and the press assumed we were back together. I hoped we were too, but I was also still angry with him. I really needed him to explain what had happened so that I could put the past behind me. But every time I tried to ask he became furious and started having a go at me.

In the evening the phone in our room kept ringing and whenever I answered it the person calling put the phone down. Then I overheard George ringing Phil.

'Tell Gina Alex is going home soon.'

It was like a red rag to a bull. 'What's it got to do with her?' I shouted. 'Tell me once and for all what's going on between you!'

'We're just friends!' he yelled back, storming out of the room.

As soon as he had gone I grabbed his mobile. Sure enough, her number was on it. Hardly able to think straight I dialled it up. As soon as she answered I let rip, calling her all kinds of names and telling her in no uncertain terms to leave my husband alone. Then I slammed the phone down. It hadn't made me feel any better. As I put George's phone back on the table I noticed a pile of papers I hadn't seen before. I picked them up, hardly believing my eyes: they were contracts between George and Gina and a newspaper.

I threw them at George when he walked back in and then a massive row kicked off. He claimed that it was simply that she was being hassled by the press and needed his help.

'What about me, your wife?' I screamed at him. 'I've been hounded by the press all because of you and when have you ever helped me?' I thought I was going mad.

We carried on screaming at each other until, at 2am, George called security to get me thrown out of the building.

I curled up in one of the chairs in reception. I felt such an emotional wreck that I was in no fit state to drive anywhere. I stayed there for an hour or so and then crept back up to the room. I got into bed next to George; the fight had gone out of both of us and he hugged me.

George was supposed to be coming home with me the next day for yet another new start, but then Mum called. She'd been told that Gina had sold her story to the *News of the World* – all about her nights of passion with George. I was still reeling from his betrayal with Paula; this was adding insult to injury. I thought the worst had happened, but every day it seemed some new torment was added. I've always been a strong person, able to cope with most things, but this was pushing me to the limit. After a succession of rows, George still refusing to admit that Gina was anything but a friend, we drove home. We'd only been in the house a matter of hours when we had yet another row – triggered by me begging him to tell me the truth about Gina – and he drove back to the health farm.

Sure enough, Gina's story about their torrid nights of

passion appeared in the *News of the World*. I couldn't bring myself to read it. I'd had some lows in our married life, but this was the lowest yet. Even after all this, George kept asking if he could come home. I repeatedly said no and then I caved in and said I would think about it. George obviously took that for a yes, because later that night he let himself into the house. I was already in bed asleep; I woke up to find George getting in to bed with me. He tried to kiss me but I pushed him away. He stank of sex. I felt total revulsion. 'I don't know where you've been. Frankly, you'd need to go in a sheep dip to be disinfected before I ever let you near me again!'

Perhaps if I had known where he had been the night before I would have kicked him out there and then, but he was rather economical with the truth, leaving it to the press to tell his side. That weekend one of the papers ran an interview with George and Gina. They were pictured together staying at a hotel in Reigate, where they had apparently spent their first night together – the night before George came back to me. He could hardly deny it now! He admitted that he had been unfaithful but swore that it wouldn't happen again. I thought bitterly, How many promises did you make about not drinking again and how many times did you break them? Right from the start of our relationship I had said that I could put up with many things, I could put up with the drinking and the gambling, but I would never put up with infidelity.

Then I received a letter from a local solicitor filing for

The move to the Flint
Barn was celebrated
with a joint birthday and
housewarming party.

Above: With my good friend Gail Porter and her former husband Dan Hipgrave. As you can see, she was heavily pregnant with her daughter at the time of the party.

Below: My dad with everyone's favourite East End girl, Barbara Windsor.

Above: When George ordered bubbly, I don't think this is what he had in mind!
Inset: With Rua when he was a puppy.

Below: On holiday in Portugal with our good friend Phil.

Main picture: Top of the class –
George receiving his honorary
Doctorate from Queen's
University in Belfast in 2001.

Inset: The Best clan pose for a
picture the day that George was
awarded the freedom of the
Borough of Castlereagh.

Jungle fever – my time on *I'm a Celebrity Get Me Out of Here* was anything but dull.

Above: I still shudder at the thought … making my way through the Tunnel of Trouble.

Below: Lord Brocket was extremely keen to help me wash off any remaining creepy crawlies afterwards.

Inset: Free at last. With my sister Jo, outside the luxury Versace hotel in Australia, after being voted off the show.

Main picture: I was asked to dress up as Marilyn for a tribute to her by the *Sunday Mirror*.

Inset: Bottoms up! I was voted Rear of the Year in 2004.

I give as much of my spare time – and energy – as I can to the charities I support.

Above: Terrified, but determined, before my parachute jump in aid of AIDS 2000.

Below left: On the Playtex Moonwalk, walking in aid of Breakthrough Breast Cancer.

Below right: Climbing Mount Kilimanjaro in aid of the Childrens Trust.

A publicity shot from the time I spent presenting on *This Morning*. Since leaving George, I've been able to pursue my own career and love the work I've been doing. Onwards and upwards!

divorce and citing my unreasonable behaviour as grounds: I apparently drank too much, was intolerable to live with, was unfaithful … and, to top it all, I practised voodoo! I thought that if I really had done the latter, there were a few people who wouldn't have been around any more! It would have been funny if I hadn't felt so hurt. Even George must have realised he'd gone too far, and got the solicitor to withdraw the proceedings.

But he was still losing himself in drink, spending some of the time in our house and the rest at the health farm. And we were still being pursued by the press – hardly surprising, I suppose, given George's lurid revelations and erratic behaviour. I was having to find out what was going on in my life by opening a newspaper as they seemed to know more about what George was up to than I did. George punched another photographer and fractured his hand, so I ended up taking him to hospital. Then he punched yet another photographer, this time with his uninjured hand. The saga of BestEnders continued to unfold in the tabloids. I was finding the press attention unbearable. Once I even had to call the police when a photographer managed to take a picture of me getting out of the shower. It was shocking feeling that my privacy was being invaded like this. Another time, as I drove back to Forest Mere to drop off George's things, I stopped off to buy some petrol and seven other cars pulled over.

I'd finally had enough. At the end of September, after enduring weeks of emotional turmoil, I announced our separation. It wasn't something I did lightly, but I really didn't think I could go on like this and I saw it as one way of ending the media circus. If we weren't together I hoped they would leave us alone. I wish I had walked away once and for all then, but George hadn't quite managed to crush all the love out of me and when he begged me again to take him back in mid-October, claiming to have called off his affair with Gina, I said yes.

He had stopped drinking, but hadn't fully moved back home yet. He would still pop back to Forest Mere, saying that it helped him to keep off the bottle and that he wanted to use the gym. He didn't seem that committed to our marriage, though – I think he secretly liked having his single life at Forest Mere and knowing that I was waiting back at home for him.

We went to France with his sister Barbara and her husband Norman and ended up deciding to buy a holiday villa with them. For a few days things were calm between us, but I wouldn't say we were close. Then I went with him to Dublin, where he was interviewed on a TV chat show. He confessed that he'd been a pig to me, that he was sorry, that he still loved me and wanted our marriage to survive.

We said we wanted to give it another go, but looking back I don't think my heart was in it. I felt I was putting more effort into the marriage than he was, even though I was the wronged party and couldn't trust him any more. I was constantly checking his phone to see who he had rung or texted. It was such a horrible, insidious feeling. I felt on edge all the time. I couldn't relax around him and I certainly didn't trust him enough to make love with him.

There was an uneasy truce between us. One Saturday night, when George was at one of his inevitable stays at Forest Mere and I was at a neighbour's party, my agent called with some shocking news. The *News of the World* had just rung him to say that they were running a story that Gina was pregnant by George. Somehow I managed to leave the party and get back home. I called George, who once more was full of denials. Logically, I knew that it was very unlikely that she could be pregnant because of George's low fertility levels, but that didn't stop the hurt and the doubt creeping in. What if she was? Pregnancy had been my long-held dream for George and me. I phoned my parents in floods of tears. They wanted to come over straight away, but I said I was going to bed.

In the morning my dad came round to check up on me. I heard him knocking and got up. I felt totally light-headed, emotionally and physically shattered, and as I walked down the stairs I lost my footing and fell head-first on the slate floor below, knocking myself unconscious. My poor dad was beside himself as the door was locked from the inside. He finally managed to break it down with the help of a neighbour – by now blood was pouring from a deep cut on my forehead – and rush me to hospital, where I needed several stitches. It wasn't the physical pain that I cared about, though.

Throughout the summer and early autumn I had felt as if I was drowning in pain and misery, feeling totally out of control and helpless. I had been with George for nine years and I couldn't imagine life without him. By November, however, my survival instinct had finally kicked in. George and I were living together again, but I was beginning to feel that things could never be the same between us again. There were even news stories circulating that he was seeing other women at Forest Mere. Every other Sunday the papers would link him to yet another blonde – each new one a clone of the last. One Sunday in November George called me from the health farm reminding me to put my clocks back. It wasn't the kind of thing he usually did. As soon as I opened the Sunday papers I knew why he'd done it. One of George's blondes had sold her story. She revealed how they had foreplay in his Mini Cooper and sex on the pool table and how he had put her up in a hotel just minutes away from where I lived. George had obviously called me to see if I had read the story. I knew he'd only deny it if I rang him back. I was so sick of all the lies, numb from his betrayals.

The trust had gone and I came to the conclusion that I couldn't forgive the past. In fact, instead of letting my life revolve around his and waiting for him to come back to me, I was starting to build a life of my own at last. I socialised more and I enjoyed the freedom of being able to go out with whom I wanted, when I wanted, without having to answer to anyone else. I also received more offers of work and took on a number of modelling jobs. I wasn't going to sit at home and feel like a victim any more.

It was around this time that I was invited to appear on *I'm a Celebrity... Get Me Out of Here!*. Initially I was sceptical and didn't think it was for me. But I found myself enjoying the interview and when they asked me to make up my mind I said yes. I reasoned that I had nothing to lose – compared to the year I'd just been through, spending two weeks in the jungle, even if it might involve eating witchety grubs and swimming in snake-infested pools, would be a picnic in the park!

In November I was asked to model for *Loaded*. In fact, I was going to be the cover girl, in a gorgeous gold bikini. Not bad going for a 31-year-old, I thought – ancient in modelling terms! Maybe something good had come out of the emotional roller coaster I'd been on after all – the weight had fallen off me, and I was down to a size 6.

I decided I needed a night away before the shoot, so I booked a room at the Berkeley for my friend Julie and me. We were in the middle of having dinner when I received a call from a drunken George. He had just fallen into the fish pond in our garden and had lost his door keys. I raised my eyebrows at Julie and shook my head. I told him I was sorry but I'd had a few drinks and couldn't get back to sort him out. I was sick to death of having to drop everything when he needed me to. He phoned back a few minutes later to say he'd found the keys. God knows how he'd fallen in the pond anyway – it had a fence round it.

The magazine also wanted to interview me, and so a couple of days after the shoot I met Martin, the editor, and Dean, the journalist, for lunch. We all got on famously, much wine flowed and lunch became the evening before I realised what the time was. When I finally switched on my phone I had sixty messages from George, furiously demanding where I was, each getting progressively more aggressive and threatening.

I walked into our kitchen and let out a gasp of horror. George had smashed the stereo on the stone floor and strewn papers and CDs everywhere.

'What the hell have you done?' I cried.

'Where have you been?' he shouted back angrily, and then started accusing me of having an affair.

Not wanting a row, I took myself off to bed. The next day I felt a little hungover and pottered around the house, nursing my sore head. By the afternoon I was feeling better and planned to pick up the dogs from my mum's. George said that he had to go out as well to collect his car and that he had a taxi coming.

'Well, I'll see you later,' I said, about to leave.

'Can't you wait till I've gone?' he said.

'No, I've got to go now.'

God, he's infuriating sometimes, I thought, ignoring him and walking to the garage. I was about to switch on the engine when I noticed that the heavy stone doorstop that was usually by our front door was lying on the passenger seat. Suddenly I became aware of how cold it was in the car. I turned round, and gasped in disbelief – the entire back windscreen had been smashed. I got out of the car and walked around it – every single panel of my lovely Mercedes had been kicked and beaten in. 'George!' I shouted, storming back to the house. But George had fled, leaving the front door wide open. In the distance I saw a taxi pull up and George sneak out of the bushes and get into it. I was absolutely livid about such wanton destruction of my property, but also quite scared. He'd obviously been in a completely drunken rage when he'd done it. It was back to the bad old days with a vengeance – a time I had no intention of returning to.

To my relief, he didn't come home that night. The following morning I opened the paper and found out exactly where he'd been. My husband had spent the night with two prostitutes. I don't think I had any more tears left to cry. I sat there reading the story over and over again, in a complete state of shock. Did I mean so very little to him that he would do this? Was this his final way of driving me away once and for all, leaving him free to drink himself into oblivion?

Apparently he had picked up the prostitutes and taken them to a hotel. Once there he'd given one of them money to go and buy a camera to take some pictures but the pair of them had robbed him. He was photographed sitting in reception in a dressing gown, waiting for the police – a pitiful sight. There was no way things could ever be the same between us again. I didn't even know this man any more. His personality had changed; his behaviour was so extreme, it was as if he was a different person.

He didn't call. Phil told me that he was back staying with Gina, and by now the papers had reported that she'd had a miscarriage. I don't quite know what possessed me, but early one morning I woke up at six and thought, I just have to see for myself what's going on there. My car was being repaired, so I had a hire car that neither George nor Gina would recognise. I drove to her council estate and sat in the car for a minute or two, staring up at the house, wondering if George was there. Then I got out and knocked on the door. A bottle-blonde head peered out of the window at me. I knew that Gina's curiosity would get the better of her and after a few minutes she opened the door. Bizarrely, she acted as if it was the most natural thing in the world that I, the wife of her lover, should be standing on her doorstep. She immediately asked me in for a cup of coffee.

'Did you hear about the prostitutes, then?' she asked, almost gleefully. It was obvious that she was loving every second of being with George, regardless of what he did, because he was famous. Now she had her fifteen minutes.

'Is he here, by any chance?' I asked.

'No he ain't,' she replied. But as I could see his bag lying on the side, I didn't exactly believe her.

I said I needed to use her bathroom and she directed me upstairs. As I made my way there I wrinkled my nose from the strong smell of cats, which seemed to be everywhere, and couldn't help noticing the gerbil cage in the bath. There was a small door leading from the bathroom. Knowing exactly who would be behind there, I pushed it open and walked into the poky bedroom. George was lying on the bed. He was naked and surrounded by around ten empty wine bottles. It was obviously Gina's bedroom; an overflowing ashtray was on the bedside table and her make-up was on the dressing table.

I looked at him for a few minutes, took a deep breath, then said, 'Right, that's it then.'

He looked sheepish, but didn't bother to say anything. He could hardly talk himself out of this one, could he? Then I turned and ran out of the house, got into my car and drove home. I had seen for myself how low he had sunk. The image of him lying there was one I would never forget.

My marriage was over. I knew it once and for all. I had given George so many chances. I couldn't give him any more.

CHAPTER SIXTEEN
I WILL SURVIVE

I had truly believed that George was the love of my life. I had done all I could to hold on to that love, but no more. I couldn't – wouldn't – be dragged down to his level. For those three years when he had been ill I had known almost complete happiness with him and I wasn't going to stand by and watch him destroy both himself and me. I had been with him for nine years. I had thought we would be together forever, I had hoped we would have a family. All my dreams had been shattered. It was time to walk away.

Leaving him was the hardest thing I've ever had to do. But I had to do it. It was either that or stay for more of the same: more heartbreak, more abuse, more lies, more betrayals and with no hope that things would ever get better. I didn't want to find myself in the position of being forty years old and discovering that I'd left it too late for meeting someone else, too late for having children, too late to start again. George had made his choice. He had chosen drink. Now I had to choose life.

He kept calling me, leaving endless messages – the all-too-familiar ritual of saying sorry, and begging me to let him come back. But I didn't speak to him. I had nothing left to say. By now I had a solicitor to act on my behalf in the divorce proceedings, and we were trying to arrange a meeting with George and his solicitor – what's called a 'without prejudice' meeting – to see if we could divorce amicably. Even after everything he had put me through I still didn't want things to be acrimonious between us.

But George wasn't going to leave my life that easily. One night I woke up suddenly and went downstairs to check on the dogs. Rua came as soon as I called him, but, unusually, Red wasn't in the house. I went out to the garden, calling for him but he still didn't come. Feeling increasingly worried, I ran back inside and searched for my mobile but that was missing too. I quickly realised the most likely explanation – George still had the keys to the house and must have let himself in and taken Red. I phoned him and he admitted that he had Red. I was furious but knew there was no point in having a go at him if I wanted to get my dog back, so I kept a lid on my anger.

'Please look after him and make sure he's got some water,' I simply asked him. He muttered that he would.

First thing in the morning, I rang my solicitor and he called George requesting that he return the dog and the phone immediately. George claimed to have taken my phone by mistake, saying that it had accidentally fallen into his bag.

'Did the dog accidentally fall into his bag too then?' my solicitor asked, adding one element of humour to the whole sorry affair.

We might have tried to keep things amicable but with George's erratic, irrational behaviour, I never knew what was going to happen next. I changed the locks, as I really didn't like the thought of him letting himself into the house while I was sleeping and perhaps planning another little surprise for me...

I felt devastated that my marriage was over, emotionally shell-shocked by all that had happened, but I think I must be a survivor and quite tough because somewhere I found the strength to pick myself up and start rebuilding my life. My family and friends were a great source of support and comfort to me during this very difficult time – in fact I don't know what I would have done without them. They were my crutch, my shoulder to cry on, always there for me when I needed to talk about George and I did, endlessly. I had a lot of baggage to offload about the last few months. They were disgusted by George's infidelity, totally disillusioned with him.

On a practical level, they made sure I had no shortage of invitations to go out – the last thing I wanted to do was to stay at home on my own. In mid-December my very good friend Gail Porter invited me to a party. As I drove along the Kings Road to her house I saw a familiar figure staggering out of Pucci's. It was George. He was obviously drunk. I half thought about driving on; hadn't I spent enough time dealing with a drunken George? Then I realised I had to stop. I pulled over and got out of the car.

'Are you OK George?'

He tried to focus on me. He looked terrible: drunk, dishevelled, unshaven.

'No I'm not,' he replied. 'Please can I come home?'

A few months before, I would have crumbled and taken him back without hesitation. But too much had happened since then.

'I'm really sorry George, but I'm on my way somewhere. I'm sorry. Take care of yourself.'

I felt awful driving off and leaving him in that state. But I had given up everything for him once and it hadn't worked; I knew it wouldn't again. However, as it grew closer to Christmas, I had the strongest feeling that I would be spending it with George. In spite of everything I still couldn't bear to think of him being on his own, drinking Christmas away in the Phene and staying alone in some anonymous hotel.

There was no way I could expect my parents to have George over for Christmas, they couldn't even have stayed in the same room as him after his treatment of me. So I got in supplies for a Christmas dinner for two. A couple of days before Christmas as I was getting the last of my shopping in Harrods I got the phone call I had been expecting and half dreading. It was a friend of George's from the Phene Arms to say that George was in a very bad state and asking if I could pick him up.

As I walked into the pub, I thought, this really is the last time I ever want to do this. George was paralytic, but somehow I managed to get him into the car and drive him home. On the way back, I had to call in at mum and dad's to collect the dogs.

'Just be civil,' I implored them both. Dad left the house, not wanting any more scenes.

George cried when he saw the dogs – perhaps he really was crying because he had missed them or perhaps they were tears because he knew he had thrown away his marriage. Or perhaps he was too drunk to know. It was heartbreaking seeing him like this. He was such a pitiful sight.

We'd had some rocky times in the past over Christmas when his drinking had been out of control, but he surpassed himself this time, drinking non-stop. The house was rapidly littered with empty wine bottles – he obviously still had supplies stashed there from the summer. I was back to my role of looking after him and cooking him food. I wasn't expecting gratitude but I hoped at least things could be civilised between us. Some hope. On Christmas Eve night I was repeatedly woken up by his mobile phone. It rang constantly until four in the morning. I could even hear it from the spare room where I was sleeping – George had crashed out in my bed. I expected it was one of his women trying to get hold of him and it did make me angry.

On Christmas Day morning I went round to Mum

and Dad's to hand out my presents and see all the family. Everything there was so happy and so normal; I longed to stay with them. But after a few hours, I returned home with a heavy heart to carry on my farce of a Christmas Day. George was lying in bed drinking wine and I got on with making Christmas dinner. I just wanted the day to be over. But, after our sad meal for two, an almighty row broke out between us. His phone had continued to ring and finally I had snapped. I let out all the rage that had been building up over his appalling treatment of me.

We were screaming at each other, shouting out insults and accusations and then George lost it. He punched me in the face. I fell back and he pinned me down and continued to hit me and pull my hair. I was terrified. We'd had fights in the past but nothing as bad as this. He seemed out of control, beyond reason. I seriously thought that he might kill me or that I might end up killing him in self-defence. In desperation I hit out at his face, but that had no effect. Struggling frantically I managed to punch him in the balls and I was able to free myself. He obviously realised that he had gone too far this time and took himself off to his snug. Panting and shaking, tasting the blood from my split lip I phoned the police. Even though George now looked subdued I was still terrified of being in the same house as him.

Some fifteen minutes later the police arrived. It was such a relief to see them; I just wanted the nightmare to end. I sat curled up on the sofa, wrapped in a blanket, shaking from the shock and pain of it all.

'Don't look now,' one of the officers warned, 'We're going to arrest George and bring him through the house.'

I hid my face in my hands as they walked by. I hated to think of him being locked in a police cell but he had left me with no other choice.

While George was driven away to the police station, one of the other officers drove me to my parents. Even though they had been expecting something like this to happen, they were still horrified by my bruised and battered face.

The following day, two detectives came round to interview me. They tried to persuade me to press charges against George. But I refused. For me his arrest was punishment enough. I didn't want to prolong the agony.

I spent the next few weeks at my parents'. I really couldn't face the house – that final scene between us had been so awful and I dreaded returning there. I didn't speak to George or hear from him. Even he must have realised that our marriage was finally over and that there was no going back. I knew he wouldn't forgive me for having him arrested. I heard that he moved back in with Gina. But he must have felt guilty about what he'd done because he wrote to my parents trying to give his version of the event. Tellingly, he made no attempt to apologise but implied that what had happened had been my fault. But that's alcoholics for you – attack is always the best form of defence and whatever they've done, they always try to shift the blame to the other person.

When I finally felt up to going back home, mum and dad had to stay with me. I needed to lay those ghosts to rest and was in no state to be left on my own. But it wasn't easy being at home – George had barely taken anything apart from his clothes and everywhere I looked was a reminder of our marriage, of the life we had together – the pictures, the ornaments, even the furniture – we had bought everything together and every time I looked at our possessions I wanted to weep. I felt very low. I knew I had done the right thing leaving my marriage, but I still felt so lost.

Psychologically, I was helped by the fact that it was the end of 2003. I thought, I've got a new year a head of me, it's time to try and put the past behind me - my marriage is irretrievable, there's no going back now, no last chances to make it work, it's over and somehow I've got to accept that and move on. So much easier said than done...

Ironically, some friends dragged me out to spend New Years Eve at Tramp, the night club where I had first met George in 1994. Ten years on, here I was at the same place and our relationship was over. I even sat at the same table as Johnny Gold, Tramp's owner and the man who had first introduced me to George all those years ago. I could have felt haunted by memories from the past but, actually, I had a fantastic time.

And, bizarrely, my imminent appearance on *I'm A Celebrity, Get Me Out of Here* in January 2004 also gave me something else to focus on and was quite good therapy in the circumstances. I can't exactly say that I prepared for it by doing any exercise – but then apart from the Bushtucker trials you don't do very much while you're there! I made sure I covered the essentials, though, by having a manicure and a pedicure and an eyelash tint as you can't take any make up with you. And, of course, I had some sunbed sessions. Yes, I admit it: 'my name is Alex and I'm a tan-aholic.' I have tried to cut back to a couple a month because I know its bad for you, but I can't give them up altogether, I loathe being white. I've given up on the fake tan because I always do a botch job and end up with hideous orange tide marks round my hands and feet. Quite a few celebrity mags have picked up on my addiction and I have been mortified to discover pictures of myself with the word 'tangoed!' printed underneath. Even more shamefully they sometimes put me in the same luminous orange category as David Dickinson or even Donatella Versace, which I think is very unfair! I swear they airbrushed me to make me look more orange. I'm actually quite lightly tanned – honest!

I was very nervous as I flew over to Australia. Suddenly I felt full of self-doubt and anxiety. I wondered whether I should have agreed to take part in the programme - it had seemed like a good idea at the time, but now I wasn't so sure. I felt that everyone else on the show had a profession and some kind of right to call themselves a 'celebrity', whereas I was just George's wife – soon to be ex-wife – and I had never seen myself as a 'celebrity'. But I tried to push those thoughts to the back of my mind. Now I was mid-air, it was a bit too late for second thoughts! I reminded myself that I wanted to try a completely different experience, something that would help me forget the misery of the past months. And after all, this was only television – I couldn't really take it that seriously!

Once I arrived at the hotel in Brisbane I only had an hour to get ready for the cocktail party – I really wanted to look good as I knew I'd be roughing it for the next couple of weeks – so I made the most of putting on make up and slipping into a lovely, thin-strapped designer dress. Then it was off to meet my fellow contestants. I was delighted to see one person I knew, Razor, the ex-footballer. We'd met through John Scales and I'd always got on well with him. Everyone else seemed lovely and on their best behaviour. Everyone, that is, except John Lydon who marched into the room, took one look at us and then walked out again! I had been looking forward to talking to him as in my teens I'd been through a bit of a punk phase and had loved the Sex Pistols.

After we had collected our jungle kit – Razor, Katie (aka Jordan) and I sneaked downstairs and had a few more drinks at the bar. It was there I found out that she and I had someone in common – John Scales. She'd been on a couple of dates with him. It's a small world, I thought to myself.

The following morning, we had to get up at six o'clock to start our jungle orientation. Actually, I overslept as I was still jet-lagged and I loathe getting up early. Our first trip was to the wildlife park, where Dr

Bob briefed us about which beasts and bugs to be prepared for in the jungle. In particular, he warned us about the poisonous spiders and venomous brown snakes and I sincerely hoped I wouldn't be meeting any of them! We also had to handle a number of creepy crawlies, including the gruesome witchety grubs, though none of us could have imagined that some of our number would end up having to eat them! The production team were very keen to find out about our likes and dislikes and I decided to lie and say I was terrified of spiders, when actually it's snakes, as I was convinced they were cunning enough to make you confront your worst nightmare. Although my worst nightmare was actually about to come true – going into the jungle and not being able to take my hair dryer and straightening irons. I need them on a daily basis and I was absolutely dreading my hair going curly! I have to take my hat off to Katie, getting her hair braided was a stroke of genius as I gather she also has a horror of frizzy hair. Never mind the poisonous snakes there is nothing to beat a bad hair day!

After a further day spent learning how to tie knots and use a compass, endless press interviews plus a very pleasant barbecue thrown by Peter Andre's parents, we were finally helicoptered into the jungle. The first little surprise the production team had in store for us was that we had to make our beds and we were one bed short – someone was going to have to sleep in the hammock. In the end, Peter very kindly volunteered to take it. Luckily for me, Brocket was a whizz with knots thanks to his army training; I can't imagine any bed made by me would have lasted very long.

Although we had all been issued with a nightshirt, I had no intention of taking my clothes off – there were far too many bugs and beasts around and no escape from the cameras! So I went to bed fully clothed and zipped my sleeping bag completely over my head. It was hideously hot in my nylon cocoon but I'd rather roast than be bitten by something nasty. In fact, on our very first night in the jungle we had a close encounter. I woke up to Razor shouting, 'Snake!' and pointing at Kerry's bed. Sure enough, there was a massive brown snake under her bed – the poisonous variety we had been warned about. Kerry, bless her, was so petrified she couldn't move and meanwhile the snake assumed the striking position. Luckily Razor came to the rescue and ran over, picked her up and whisked her away, what a hero.

I've no idea what time we got up the next day as we weren't allowed to take our watches with us – even when we had to get the batteries changed for our microphones by the production crew, they had tape over their watches. Because we had no idea what the time was, we probably went to bed at seven o'clock, when it got dark because there was nothing else to do!

From day one I was the chef, a role that I was happy to take on partly because I love cooking and partly because it gave me something to do. But it was a bit of a thankless task. Our basic rations were rice and dried beans and it took us nearly a week to realise that we had to soak the beans first! We were all hungry, nearly all the time, and spent a lot of time discussing our food fantasies. In fact, even when people won enough stars in the Bushtucker Trials there would never be enough food to go round and anyway it was never particularly appetising. Once, we were rewarded with a single chicken for the ten of us, with its head and feathers still on! Another time it was one large ostrich egg. When we were given a wombat to look after, Johnny confiscated its food and we ended up making a revolting stew with its nuts and sweetcorn – that's how hungry we were. It was either that or eat the wombat, which Johnny threatened to do, thought I don't think that would have gone down very well with the British public! We held her hostage, though, and only gave her back when we were given some chocolate brownies.

I know the programme-makers and viewers were probably hoping that there would be major personality clashes and fiery arguments but in fact we all got on extremely well and I liked everybody. Peter Andre was a sweet guy, Katie was lovely, very open and nice and not what I had been expecting. She also very kindly plaited my hair for me every day, so I didn't have to be on TV with the dreaded curls – for which I am eternally grateful. Kerry was a sweetie, she said she saw me as her older sister and I felt very protective towards her; Jennie was good fun and I admired her for her determination to play the game; Diane was quiet but very warm; Mike was a really nice guy and was the one who kept us entertained at night, by getting us to put on musicals and charades. Our *Oliver Twist* was a triumph, but I don't think it was ever shown. Johnny was mad at times, but always entertaining and quite often I would sit on his camp bed at night sharing his last remaining cigarettes – and we'd talk about the Sex Pistols. Sid Vicious had been my absolute idol so it was wonderful, if not a little surreal being able to ask Johnny all about him. He told me how talented he had been and how tragically self-destructive and I thought, That reminds me of a certain person... Overall, I bonded most with Brocket. He's very charismatic, charming, funny, a little mad and full of fascinating stories.

I found myself quickly having fun, and getting into the spirit of the adventure, my anxieties on the plane forgotten. It was actually quite therapeutic to be away and it was certainly a break from reading the papers and discovering what my husband had been up to or receiving nasty text messages from him. I felt happier and calmer than I had in a long time.

I celebrated my 32nd birthday in the jungle, but if we were hoping for a lavish party to be laid on we were going to be disappointed. Rather than being presented with a delicious cake, I was simply given the ingredients to make my own - fortunately it was chocolate so that cheered us up. As I blew out the candles I remember wishing for a happier and less eventful year – I felt I'd had enough drama to last me a lifetime. We were only given two bottles of wine between ten of us, though actually just one glass went straight to my head as I was so hungry and I would rather have had a nice cup of tea! It certainly goes down as one of my more memorable birthdays – watching everyone playing charades, dressed in different scraps of leopard skin is an image that will stay with me for some time!

I had been in the jungle for around five days and I was dying to do a Bushtucker trial. I suppose I wanted to prove to myself that I could do one and it would be a welcome change from the monotony of sitting around the camp fire but when the moment came I was extremely nervous.

'Right then Alex, your trial is called "The Tunnel of Trouble."' Ant and Dec grinned away at me. I managed a feeble smile back. I'd wanted to do this after all. I had five Perspex compartments to crawl through on my hands and knees, collecting two stars from each using my mouth and attaching them to the magnets on the side of the glass. Of course, the compartments weren't empty. The first one contained thirty squirming eels. I hate fish but I managed to collect the two stars even when one bit me on the nose. Next I had to contend with mealworm larvae and maggots. I nearly gagged from the smell – it was like rotting flesh – and I got covered in filthy slime. Then it was on to spiders and cockroaches. I'm not too worried about spiders, though I didn't particularly want to get bitten by a huntsman. One was sitting one of the stars, I tried blowing it off but it wouldn't budge and in the end I had to pick up the star, spider and all. I was spurred on by the thought of my hungry campmates. Next came ostrich feathers full of mites and lice, which of course stuck to my slimy body, making me resemble Big Bird!

The final cage was stuffed with snakes. I really am petrified of these. When I was on holiday in Kenya with my parents aged eleven, a deadly green mamba flew out of a tree towards me and the locals quickly killed it with their machetes. I knew that none of the snakes in the cage would be deadly but I really didn't like the way they had all assumed the s-bend striking position. I decided I really wasn't going to be bitten for the sake of half a carrot and so uttered the essential words, 'Get me out of here!'

I emerged with eight stars – we would eat that night! But I looked, felt and smelled disgusting, I was covered in cockroaches and slime and I was itching all over from the mites. I had never wanted a shower more. They were all pretty stunned by the state of me when I arrived back at the camp.

Brocket took charge. 'Come on, girl, I'll give you a good old scrub,' he said taking me to the pool and helping me strip off. At that point I really didn't care about the cameras; I just wanted to be clean. Brocket did indeed give me a good scrub down, leaving no part of me untouched, particularly my backside! Yes, I probably should have worn a more substantial pair of pants than a thong but I didn't know I'd be showing it off to millions of viewers. But then I can't really complain as that footage helped me win Rear of the Year! Later, George was to send me a text congratulating me on winning 'arsehole of the year' – how very charming.

I was the fifth person to be voted out, coming very respectably in the middle and, by then, I was delighted. The novelty had worn off and we were all getting very hungry and very bored and I was thinking enviously of my sister lounging around in the luxurious Versace hotel. Apart from the trials, there simply isn't enough to occupy you and, while the rest of the nation was gripped by the unfolding story of Katie's flirtation with Peter, we weren't really aware of what was going on, apart from one night when Jennie alerted us to the fact that Peter wasn't in his hammock! It's a pity we didn't know more, as it might have distracted us from thinking about food incessantly. I had great fun though, it was definitely a laugh and it was good to have a break from brooding about my failed marriage. But more importantly, I had raised £123,000 for The Children's Trust, which specialises in caring for children who are severely disabled and I was proud about that.

When I came out I heard that George had been done for drink driving – thank God, I thought, I don't have to deal with that any more. He had returned to making his after-dinner speeches and at one I heard he made some joke about me being in the jungle and how a snake bit me and the snake died. I might have wished him well but he didn't seem to feel the same about me.

Back home, I discovered that my cleaner had let George into the house when I had been in the jungle. For some bizarre reason he had stolen a pot of my Crème de Mer face cream. I don't imagine it was for him to use –

perhaps he had given it to one of his girlfriends. Though quite what they made of having a second-hand pot of cream, albeit a very expensive one, is anybody's guess. Yet again I had to get my locks changed; I really didn't want George letting himself into the house unannounced. My cleaner left my employment after that, angry with me because I hadn't given her a Christmas bonus and ended up telling a journalist a story about me, saying how nasty I was to George! Talk about being taken to the cleaners! I was livid. Fortunately I had just started writing a column for *Closer* magazine and was able to say how ridiculous her accusations were.

On top of that, I had a phone call from Gina. She actually had the cheek to ask me for advice on how to deal with George! She said he was driving her mad with his drinking.

He's your problem now,' I told her, amazed that she'd had the nerve to phone me. Then she said that she'd voted for me when I was in the jungle. Was I supposed to be grateful, I wondered? You have an affair with my husband, but I'll forgive you because you make one phone call? I was so glad to be out of George's chaotic world. By now I had officially filed for divorce on the grounds of his adultery.

But now I had to get used to living on my own and it was a huge adjustment. My life had revolved around George and it took me a long time to feel comfortable being on my own. I desperately missed being married. I missed the companionship, I missed sharing things with my husband, missed being close to him, missed going to bed with him and waking up with him in the morning. George had been everything to me – my lover, my soul mate, my best friend and we had done everything together. Whenever he had a job I went with him – throughout our marriage we had barely been apart. I felt as if I had lost my right arm.

Now I was single and at times I felt terribly lonely. Everything I did reminded me of what I had lost – if I went food shopping, I hated looking at the purchases in my trolley – pathetic reminders that I would just be cooking for one. I missed looking after George, missed cooking for him – all my attention had been focused on him and I found it hard to look after myself. I often had to make a real effort to eat properly, it was easier to have a glass of wine and a slice of toast.

But it wasn't just George I missed. Phil, his agent, had been one of my closest friends but now the split between George and me was final, Phil would have nothing to do with me. I had also been extremely close to George's family but, with the exception of George's dad, none of the others seemed to want to know me. In January I had rung Carol, his sister, to explain what had happened and she was very aloof with me. She had obviously decided that sides needed to be taken. A pity, because we had got on very well and I had hoped we would always be friends.

George had also been my full-time job – as well as his wife I'd been his PA and his nurse and it did seem strange not running around after him any more. I felt I needed to find my niche. I also urgently needed to find a way of earning some money because George left without giving me a penny and with a mortgage to pay. I did some more TV presenting which I enjoyed and more modelling for various men's mags, thinking I'm only young once, I may as well flaunt it, then I can look back in twenty years time and say 'Wow, I didn't used to look too bad!'. I also modelled for various cosmetics and for a fake-tan product– obviously my tan addiction was well known!

I also started writing a column for *Closer* magazine, sharing my views on the latest celebrity goings-on. On the work front things seemed to be looking up and working gave me more confidence, made me feel that I wasn't just someone's wife, soon-to-be-ex-wife. Also, after so many years of marriage I wanted to be financially independent and get my own career going. My sister Jo and I began to talk seriously about opening a boutique together, selling designer clothes and I felt excited about the prospect of running my own business, especially one which dealt with my very favourite products!

My personal life also started to look a little brighter. I had met someone early in the year and now I was back from Australia I began to see more of him. He was called Howard and was attractive, funny, kind… and sober. I can't say that I fell head over heels in love at first sight, but after everything I had been through it was reassuring to meet someone who seemed such a genuinely nice guy. I think we were drawn together because we were both going through divorces. His was particularly acrimonious, with his wife throwing in all kinds of nasty accusations against him, none of which I believed.

For a while, the relationship was just what I needed. As well making grand romantic gestures such as whisking me off to Paris for Valentine's weekend, he was also incredibly caring. For the first time in a relationship I felt I was with a man who I could rely on totally. He wasn't going to go AWOL on a drunken binge, or run after other women. He made me feel loved and protected and was a great source of strength to me when George texted me vindictive messages or on those days when I felt blue. I realised that not all relationships had to be as intense and unpredictable as the one I'd known with George.

Howard also looked after me, and helped me sort out my chaotic paperwork, and my finances – I'd been very good at managing George but was a total disaster when it came to my own affairs and with my impending divorce I needed to be on top of things.

In April 2004, George and I got our Decree Nisi – the first stage of our divorce proceedings. When we received the letter I think we were both shocked – this really was the end of our marriage. He called me in tears, unable to believe that it was finally over. I cried too, for our failed marriage and all my broken dreams but I knew I'd made the right decision. I knew there was nothing more I could have done for our marriage or to help George. I'm the kind of person who gives things my all and I had given the marriage and him 100%. I hate to see things fail and that's why I suppose I had taken him back for one final chance the previous summer. I had nothing more to give – he had taken it all.

And George might have cried on the phone in sadness about what he'd lost but he was also pretty unpleasant sometimes. One day in the summer, I opened a Sunday newspaper and found he had done a story comparing all his lovers and rating them out of ten for their performance in bed. He had included me with the likes of Gina and Paula and other women with whom he'd only had a one night stand – me, his wife of nine years, the woman he had said was the love of his life, the woman he said he'd be with forever. He gave me nought out of ten. I thought, How could you demean me like that?

In other interviews he came out with ludicrous accusations and slurs. I didn't respond in the press, though on one occasion I had to instruct my solicitor to act on my behalf and he secured a written apology from a newspaper. I didn't want to end up having some tit-for-tat slanging match in the media – I'd had enough of having my private life splashed in the papers. I knew none of what he said was true, but it was still upsetting seeing it there in black and white; you hope other people won't believe it, but there's always a chance they will.

I felt very frustrated that George kept being so unnecessarily vindictive – all I wanted to do was get on with my life, not be weighed down with bitterness and recriminations. Unfortunately, he wouldn't agree a financial settlement with me, which meant the divorce couldn't be finalised. I kept trying to see if we could sit down and discuss things through our solicitors to avoid going to court but George resisted all my attempts. My dream was for a clean break settlement, which would enable me to buy a place of my own – somewhere that wasn't full of memories.

CHAPTER SEVENTEEN
ALWAYS ALEX...

By the summer of 2004, even with the ongoing saga of my divorce proceedings, I was actually starting to feel much more positive about my new life without George. And though our final months together had been so traumatic and the break-up so painful, I still had no regrets about my marriage and staying with him for so many years. But now I felt I had some serious making up to do. I had spent a lot of time putting myself second in my marriage and now I wanted to do some things for myself. For the first time in a very long time I could do exactly what I wanted – I could go out clubbing with my friends, or wake up in the morning and decide to visit my friend in Spain. In the past I'd rarely gone out on my own because it made George so jealous and whenever we went away it was always because he wanted to. When we first split up I wasn't used to the freedom of being able to do what I wanted and didn't quite know how to deal with it – but after I while I started to enjoy it. I went away a lot in 2004, packing in trips to Thailand and Barbados where, memorably, I stayed at Jodie Kidd's house with my friend Dean from *Loaded,* and spent a blissful August in Spain. I relaxed in the sun and chilled out with my friends. It was liberating not being responsible for anyone but myself, free from that constant nagging worry about what George was up to.

But it wasn't all laughs in the sun. I also had some tough decisions to make about my relationship with Howard. What had started out as an easygoing romance between us had changed over the months, and it got to a point where things were becoming too serious between us – something for which I wasn't ready. I did care greatly for him but it was too soon after George, I knew I couldn't commit myself to another intense relationship. I never thought I would say this but I needed some space. Also, we were both under immense pressure from our divorce proceedings and inevitably we started arguing. I thought of all my arguments with George and I really didn't want to go down that road again. We finally parted in October 2004 on good terms and we remain very good friends. I can call him any time of day or night and he'll always be there for me.

So there I was, single for the first time in nearly fifteen years! I wanted to get out there and have some fun. I began putting more effort into my social life and for the first time in years I started going to nightclubs again and I loved it. I'd meet a group of my girlfriends for dinner, go to The Sanderson for a drink then head off to Pangea or The Embassy – and, while I wouldn't want to be hitting the clubs when I'm fortysomething – not that there's anything wrong with that. I wanted to make up for lost time. On Sundays, instead of slaving away in the kitchen and making roast dinner for George and all his cronies I could meet up with my friends at a local pub and have a long leisurely lunch with them and someone else could do the washing up!

I also began accepting invitations to premieres and launch parties – though it wasn't as if I would turn up to the opening of an envelope! These events were something of a revelation as George loathed anything like that and had always turned down any invitations in the past. At first I enjoyed getting dressed up and hitting the town to attend one of these functions but after a while I realised that I would far rather be going out with my friends. There is just so much pressure to look good, or you risk end up on the pages of some celebrity mag, having your outfit and body ripped to pieces!

'Alex, can I introduce you to someone?'
I was at The Embassy in November 2004 where I had just been modelling in a charity fashion show for SPARKS. Mark, the PR guy for the club, was steering me towards a very handsome and familiar man.

'Oh hi, I remember you from the Beckhams' party.' I smiled to myself; it was great being able to drop that line into the conversation!

'I remember you too,' he replied.

We smiled at each other. Simon Jordan, the man in question, was tall, dark, good-looking and very charismatic. We had indeed met at the Beckhams' World Cup party in 2002, when we had shared a car from the hotel to the venue. Of course, back then I was with George and he was with his girlfriend. Now we were both single. This could be interesting, I told myself. We started chatting but just as I was wondering where our conversation might lead he said he had to go.

I have to confess I felt a slight twinge of disappointment. I was in the mood for a bit of light flirtation and Simon looked as if he might fit the bill perfectly. However, just as I was leaving, Mark handed me a card with Simon's number on it – apparently he had left it for me. Well, I thought to myself on the journey back to Reigate, I've got nothing to lose if I call him.

A few days later, we were having lunch at The Wolsey – a very exclusive restaurant in Mayfair and somewhat more upmarket than the baked-potato café where I had gone on my first date with George. We got on extremely well – both enjoying the cheeky flirtatious banter that flowed easily between us. Lunch was followed by a trip to the casino where Simon handed me some money and told me to enjoy myself. I looked down and was astonished to discover that I was holding £2000! Actually, I shouldn't have been that surprised as Simon is a multi-millionaire businessman and Chairman of Crystal Palace Football Club, so two grand is probably small change to him. To me, though, it felt like a big deal and I was quite anxious about losing it at the roulette table. Fortunately I didn't do too badly and after a couple of hours was all set to hand back the chips to Simon.

'No, no,' he insisted, 'Keep it and treat yourself.' There were probably a few bills I could have paid but instead I did as he said, and treated myself to a rather gorgeous sheepskin coat from Joseph!

We saw quite a bit of each other over the next five months. There was an obvious attraction between us and we started meeting over intimate dinners. It wasn't long, however, before we only started seeing each other when we went to clubs as part of a group of friends. At the end of the night, though, I always went back to his hotel suite so we were definitely more than friends. Much as I enjoyed his company I don't think either of us really wanted to get serious. I had my impending divorce with George and really didn't want to involve anyone else in that. A year after I had split with him I was living in limbo. George still refused to agree a financial settlement with me and so we were headed to the court as a last resort – something I had never wanted to happen. Our case was set for March 2005 and until I got that out of the way I found it almost impossible to think about my future – I felt that only once the case was over could I really move on.

I also got the feeling that Simon really didn't want to be tied down or even admit to having a girlfriend, which is what I had assumed I was. Possibly it was because he hated the press attention and wanted to keep his private life strictly under wraps. I recently read an interview with him where he claimed that he saw me as 'a very good friend', but I have to say that I don't usually sleep with my very good friends or indeed accept expensive gifts from them! Rather unluckily for Simon – but luckily for me – our liaison lasted over Christmas and my birthday and I received two gorgeous presents from him – a beautiful diamond necklace from Boodle & Dunthorpe and an exquisite Patek Phillippe diamond studded watch. He also treated me to a wonderful birthday dinner at Quaglino's with a group of his and my closest friends and we managed to sink quite a few bottles of Cristal champagne. It was lovely being with such a generous man. The downside, of course, was his football connection. All those years with George hadn't done anything to make me warm to the game. I still found football an enormous yawn. I even went to a couple of matches with Simon and thought, I can't believe that here I am at yet another football match, loathing every minute of it, and having to read the programme from cover to cover again!

By February 2005 I was still wondering where I actually stood with Simon when I faced what was to be undoubtedly the biggest challenge of my life. A year earlier, The Children's Trust – the charity I had raised money for on *I'm A Celebrity, Get Me Out of Here* – asked me if I would take part in a sponsored climb of Kilamanjaro.

'I'd love to,' I replied breezily, then promptly put it to

the back of my mind. But February 2005, came around very quickly and I found myself getting ready to climb the tallest freestanding mountain in the world. I was feeling quite positive about it, reasoning that I was fit and in good shape and I would just take it slowly. But then I was warned about altitude sickness and my optimism rapidly drained away and was replaced with genuine fear.

Altitude sickness is potentially very dangerous, in some cases deadly. As you climb and the air becomes thinner you can become disorientated, violently sick, your lungs could fill with water, your blood pressure decreases and, at worst, you may lose consciousness. If that happens, you have to be rushed down the mountain as quickly as possible for urgent medical attention. I'd been imagining a pleasant expedition in beautiful surroundings, not a fight for survival! The night before we were due to set off I lay awake gripped with panic. Agreeing to do this for charity had seemed like such a good idea and now I could potentially die! The one consolation was that smokers are slightly less likely to get altitude sickness because their lungs are already used to taking in less oxygen – so that was one plus for me for not having given up yet!

It took us four gruelling days to get to the summit and four days to get back. I am enormously proud of myself for having made it. It was an endurance test and is the toughest thing I have ever done, or am ever likely to do again – I hope. It made my jungle excursion look like a picnic in the park, and if I thought I roughed it then, well that was nothing! After a day's arduous climb, we would spend the night at one of the huts along the route. There was no electricity, no washing facilities, the toilet would be a stinking hole in the ground, and the food was pretty disgusting too. But there was a great sense of camaraderie in the group and when you're faced with such a difficult situation you quickly bond with people and I struck up some good friendships.

As we walked on, the views of Kenya were stunning. But the journey became increasingly harder as it got steeper and I found it absolutely shattering walking uphill for nine hours a day. I was also still worried about altitude sickness – as we got higher, several members of our party were struck down with it and had to be stretchered down the mountain at great speed by the porters. The group leader was also concerned about me because I was hardly eating anything and they warned me that I wouldn't be able to continue with the climb unless I started to eat more. It was true, I hadn't been eating a great deal but that's because every packed lunch we had contained bananas and I loathe them. By the evening I felt slightly nauseous from climbing and didn't really feel like eating. In the morning we were given porridge and I hate milk, so I wasn't eating that either – fussy? moi? So we agreed that I would eat porridge with water and I promised them that I was keeping myself going with a stack of nutrition bars which luckily Simon had given me for the journey.

To make our final ascent, we had to set off at midnight. This was the most challenging part of the climb; it was very steep and very rocky. A party who had just made it to the summit passed as on their descent and one American guy looked at me and said, 'Welcome to hell!' Cheers mate, I thought! Yet more members of our party were affected by altitude sickness, talking gibberish, and collapsing – they were dropping like flies! I couldn't believe that so far, fingers crossed, I was OK.

Finally, we made it to the top. It was half past six in the morning and so we were there for sunrise. It was a beautiful, awe-inspiring sight. I felt totally exhilarated. I had made it. The most challenging experience of my life and I had done it. I felt as if I was on top of the world. It was the feeling of a lifetime. Then, of course, there was the small matter of getting back down...

Two days later, stinking to high heaven, with aching calf muscles and blackened and broken toenails we were finally back at the hotel drinking champagne and congratulating ourselves. As well as helping to raise a large sum for charity I'd also had the most wonderful detox! I had drunk vast quantities of water, not touched a drop of alcohol, barely smoked or indeed eaten, so was thin, and very fit – who needs health farms!

Once I returned home I felt in need of some r & r and so flew to Spain to see my friend Trudie. I also saw Simon, as he lives out there, and he took me out for dinner. It was lovely to see him, and there was still an undeniable attraction between us but my court case with George was only a few weeks away and I had to face it on my own. I decided from now on we were definitely just friends – and that's my definition of friendship, not his!

'Have you got everything Alex?'

I nodded to my sister Jo. It was Tuesday 22nd March, 2005, the morning of my court case and the first day of what was going to be a daunting – and no doubt expensive – three-day hearing. As we arrived at the family court in High Holborn I felt such a mixture of conflicting emotions. I felt dread that I was going to be cross-examined in court about my marriage. I knew I hadn't done anything wrong but somehow just appearing in court makes you feel as if you are guilty of something. I felt angry that this whole sorry affair had dragged on for so long and I was having to fight for what I believed I was entitled to and a I felt a certain amount of relief that, one way or another, we were going to come to a settlement at long last. But, most of all, I felt a deep sadness that our marriage was finally ending with us haggling over money in court in front of strangers. All the love, all the good times we had shared were going to be reduced into an argument about who got what. It wasn't the ending I would have chosen.

Before our court appearances, George and I went into separate meetings with our legal representatives. It was upsetting knowing that my husband was in the room next door, preparing to fight me in court. But just as we were preparing to go before the judge, George's barrister knocked at the door and offered us a deal. Clearly, now that the moment had come, George didn't want to go through with the court case. I imagine he was feeling as upset and nervous as I was and wanted the whole thing to be over.

Their first offer wasn't acceptable and we sent him back with our terms. Throughout the morning our barristers haggled over the deal. I knew that I was in a strong position because George wanted to settle out of court and I also knew the closer it got to lunch time the more desperate he would be for a drink and so even more anxious for the matter to be closed. By two o'clock we had reached a compromise. It was less than I had originally hoped for but I just wanted things to be sorted out so that I could get on with my life. We agreed a clean break settlement, which means that neither of us can go back on it – I receive a cash settlement from George and the barn in Reigate and George gets the Cheney Walk flat. So, ten years on, he's back to where he used to be in Chelsea with his beloved Phene round the corner. Whereas I can't wait to move on to something new.

Once we'd come to the agreement George shot off to the pub and I went to get our Decree Absolut. I paid the £30 and was told the paperwork would be with me within forty-eight hours. Somehow I wanted it to take longer – it seemed too much to take in at once.

Finally, around half past four in the afternoon, the barristers had drawn up the paperwork, which George and I both had to sign and we went into court to present it to the judge. She congratulated us for settling out of court but it seemed like a small victory. I looked at George sitting on the opposite side of the room to me, and was shocked by his appearance. He'd obviously been drinking heavily and he looked terrible. I really wanted to speak to him and tell him that there were no hard feelings, but I didn't have the chance as when the judge had finished and we got up to leave, he ran out of the room, clearly very upset.

I had an intense period of mourning after we broke up, made deeper by the fact that I was living in the marital home, whereas George had moved to a completely different environment, free from any memories or possessions. It took me a very long time to get over the break-up of my marriage and I can't help thinking that George hasn't really come to terms with what's happened and it was only when we were in court that the reality finally hit him.

Even though I was concerned for George, my overriding feeling was one of relief that we'd come to a settlement. I immediately took my barrister, solicitor and sister off for a bottle of much needed champagne to celebrate. But the next day I felt strangely flat and deflated. I'd been living for so long with court case hanging over me and I couldn't quite believe that it was all over.

I cheered up a little when Phil, George's agent called me the following day to say well done for getting it sorted and I hoped that we could be friends again as I'd missed seeing him. I told him that I had no hard feelings and bitterness about George and that I really didn't want to be at odds with him anymore. It was only the solicitors and court case that made it seem as if we were locked into a fight. I told Phil that I would help George in any way I could to get settled back into Cheyne Walk. I still care about him and now the fighting is over I really hope we can be friends.

I tried to hold on to those warm feelings towards him when I opened my Sunday papers the weekend after the court case, but it was a struggle. George had written a totally ludicrous story saying, amongst other ravings, that I had told him that I would rather commit suicide than go to court! It was a pack of lies – a concoction of his warped imagination but it left a very bitter taste. Somehow George always had to have the last word, even if it was totally mad and untrue. I hoped this was his swan song on our marriage.

I want to sell the barn as soon as possible now. I want to move closer to London, to start again, in a new place that's entirely mine.

My mum keeps encouraging me saying, 'Alex, you're only thirty three, you've got a new life ahead of you, think of it as being exciting!'

I know she's right and I do want to feel that optimism – but I don't know what my future holds. I know what I want; I want to get married again one day – this time for keeps – and have children. Even after everything I've been through, I still believe in love...

PICTURE CREDITS